Grandparents

Isabelle Meier presents a unique examination of the relationship between grandparents and grandchildren, viewed through the lens of analytical psychology. This relationship can have a huge impact on psychological development, yet it has been largely neglected in studies of the family.

Meier explores both clinical and theoretical material throughout the book. In the first part she dissects archetypal images in the intergenerational relationship, particularly as shown in fairy tales, myths and legends. From the 'wise old woman/man' to the 'wicked witch' or the 'old wizard', memories and experiences of these archetypes can be stored in the implicit memory and activated later in life. The second part looks at the processes and functions of implicit memory and examines the concept of the complex as it applies to grandparents, using Stern's studies on the present moment and intersubjective phenomena. Finally, Meier presents case studies from her own practice.

Grandparents is essential reading for Jungian analysts and psychotherapists, analytical psychologists and those in training. It will also be of interest to academics and students of Jungian studies, myth and anthropology, and readers looking to explore intergenerational family relationships.

Isabelle Meier, PhD, is a psychologist and Jungian analyst who trained at the C.G. Jung Institute in Zurich. Her work has been published widely in both books and journals and examines the subjects of imagination, intersubjectivity, complexes and archetypes. She is a member of the core editorial board of the German journal *Analytische Psychologie*.

Grandparents

Archetypal and clinical perspectives
on grandparent–grandchild
relationships

Isabelle Meier

Routledge
Taylor & Francis Group

LONDON AND NEW YORK

First published in English 2017
by Routledge
2 Park Square, Milton Park, Abingdon, Oxon OX14 4RN

and by Routledge
711 Third Avenue, New York, NY 10017

Routledge is an imprint of the Taylor & Francis Group, an informa business

This work is a translation of a work previously published in
German as: *Großeltern – Große Eltern: Archetypische und klinische
Perspektiven der Großeltern-Enkelkind-Beziehung*

© 2015 Brandes & Aspel Verlag GmbH, Frankfurt am Main,
Germany. All rights reserved.

Translated into English by the author.

British Library Cataloguing in Publication Data
A catalogue record for this book is available from the British Library

Library of Congress Cataloging in Publication Data
Names: Meier, Isabelle, 1956–
Title: Grandparents : archetypal and clinical perspectives on
grandparent-grandchild relationships / Isabelle Meier.
Other titles: Grosseltern-grosse Eltern. English
Description: 1 Edition. | New York : Routledge, 2017. | Originally
published: Frankfurt am Main : Brandes & Apsel, 2015. | Includes
bibliographical references and index.
Identifiers: LCCN 2016014346 (print) | LCCN 2016016395
(ebook) | ISBN 9781138688667 (hardback) | ISBN 9781138688674
(pbk.) | ISBN 9781315538099 (ebk) | ISBN 9781315538099
(ebook)
Subjects: LCSH: Grandparent and child. | Parent and child. |
Interpersonal relations. | Clinical child psychology.
Classification: LCC BF723.G68 M4513 2017 (print) | LCC BF723.
G68 (ebook) | DDC 155.6/46–dc23
LC record available at https://lccn.loc.gov/2016014346

ISBN: 978-1-138-68866-7 (hbk)
ISBN: 978-1-138-68867-4 (pbk)
ISBN: 978-1-315-53809-9 (ebk)

Typeset in Times New Roman
by Wearset Ltd, Boldon, Tyne and Wear

Contents

Introduction

Until my 35th birthday, I had no memories of my grandparents. That changed when I began a training analysis as part of my training in analytical psychology according to C.G. Jung. Suddenly, through the warmth of the therapist, a detailed set of memories arose, especially of my maternal grandfather.

I remembered stories and small episodes that I had all but forgotten. I remember how he sat at the window, smoking a Rössli cheroot (a brown, crooked cigar), reading the newspaper. I don't remember many words, more the scent of the wood, the smoke of the cigar, his figure and the morning light before it made his profile apparent. I heard the crackling fire in the stove and my grandmother bustling in the kitchen during the ritual reading of my grandfather's newspaper. It is a memory that upon reflection has meaning for me.

There were sensations that came to mind, and memories, such as that he had a lot of time and often played with me. I remembered that he called me a little devil when I tickled him or laughed with him. He said it lovingly and dearly. He gave meaning to my actions and my way of dealing with him; one that said it's good, what you do, and you can do what I like. The Jungian Jean Knox calls this self-efficacy (Knox, 2012), a feeling that is central to the development of identity. He sometimes played the game 'Knock, knock, how many fingers are on your back?' with me. I had to guess how many fingers he placed on my back. I loved this game, and so did he. It was a simple game, but one with a respectful physical contact of each other, and at the same time it deepened my bodily perception in dealing with another person. He also took me into his small apiary in which hung a measuring stick. He marked with a small pencil stub how much I had grown in a year.

That is how I spent many weeks of school vacation with my grandparents until about the time of puberty, when a new world started for me.

I thought no more of him and spent my vacations with my peers. My grandparents were also getting older, and my grandfather died as I started university. His death did not really affect me, so I forgot him completely. He was no longer a part of my life. During my studies and later at work he lost his meaning for me.

Only the care of the therapist activated these mental images and memories in the implicit memory. It could have been someone else, but it was through him. Suddenly, my maternal grandfather was before me as a mental image; but not only that, the activated memories brought a new understanding with them. This mental image of my grandfather had an expansive effect on my thinking, perceptions and feelings, as due to this something changed in the depths of my being. I am grateful to the therapist that he awoke this memory. It was something I had already experienced, but had forgotten. The Jungian Jean Knox speaks of diverse self-interests that result according to the experience of the self with people and the subsequent internalization of these relationship patterns. She says: 'There is no unifying centre of consciousness or the unconscious, but diverse selves each of which may become the focus depending on the context' (Knox, 2012, p. 455).

I also suspect that I experienced with my grandfather *moments of meeting* in accordance with the psychoanalyst Daniel Stern (Stern, 2004); moments that were full of meaning for me and influenced my perceptions, thoughts, actions and feelings in a new way. I do not think this is only possible through grandparents. Moments of meeting are possible with anyone, assuming that the conditions arise for them. I also suspect that I saw him as a *wise old man*, simply because he stood above the matter, no longer had to work, had time and was much older than my parents.

A generation takes on average 30 years, so grandparents are on average 60 years older than the grandchild. This period cannot be understood as a child; it is beyond the child's conception of time. Grandparents are the parents of the parents. This gives them more power, sometimes even magical powers for young children who are still at the magical age. They have experienced more than the parents; they are often no longer working, but are on their 'long vacation'; they no longer have to deal with the conflicts that arise in everyday life, at work and in the raising of children. That was the case for me. While my mother was busy with five children, and my father with his business, he had time. In many studies of grandparents, this is mentioned again and again: they have time.

But not only *my grandfather* was important for me. When I told my colleagues about my book project, I surprisingly often heard the phrase 'I am also a grandfather-child', 'My grandmother was central in my life', and similar expressions. In my practice as a Jungian analyst I started some time ago, by anamneses, to include the grandparent level, and asked my clients about their relationships with them. Since everyone has grandparents, memories, mental images or fantasized notions of grandparents always exist and exert a more or less strong effect, which can flow into the psychotherapy and analysis.

This book is therefore devoted to the relationship between grandparent and grandchild, and it investigates the question of what constitutes the special in this relationship. It is no coincidence that there are many descriptions of this relationship in fairy tales, legends, myths and epics (see Chapter 3). In these narratives, archetypal images and symbols are mentioned which are attributed to the grandparents as the 'wise old woman', the 'wicked witch', the 'old wizard' or the 'wise old man'.

Since this book is written with a Jungian perspective according to the analytical psychology of C.G. Jung, first the current state of research and the mentioned archetypes are defined (Chapter 1): can one define archetypes through biological, cultural, developmental psychology or ontologically? The present discussion, as it takes place mainly in the English-speaking world, is explained here. The individual can experience the archetype only as archetypal images or symbols (Chapter 2) who appear in cultural products such as the fairy tale (the 'witch', for example). Depending on the environmental situation, such archetypal image may emerge in relevant experiences with grandparents. Memories of grandmothers who were remembered as a 'wise old woman' or experienced as a 'witch' can be stored in the implicit memory as meaningful and are activated depending on the situation.

In another chapter a closer look is taken at these storage processes in implicit memory. Several models are made available in the research literature. On the one hand, the concept of 'inner working models' (Bowlby) is mentioned – which contains representative information on patterns of relationship and caregivers; on the other hand, the Jungian concept of the theme 'complex' will be addressed. Just as there is a mother complex, inferiority complex or an authority complex, the grandparent complex can also arise when dealing with grandparents. Important in this context are the studies by Daniel Stern (2000, 2004) and his research group, which indicate the importance of the presence of moments and the intersubjective phenomena, in which the inner working models or complexes can regroup.

How this happens will be described in another chapter. Based on a story and a tale of a grandchild with a grandparent ('Heidi' and 'Red

Riding Hood') it will be shown how a present moment can arise that activates the inner working models or complexes (Chapter 5). The parties develop, according to this specific moment, in a completely different direction, so we speak here of an archetypal present moment.

In Chapter 6, a digression on the current importance of the grandparent–grandchild relationship is offered. The literature about the grandparent–grandchild relationship has grown rapidly in recent years. Attempts are being made to present the reasons from a social scientific perspective and to provide outlines of the meaning of grandparents' developmental psychology.

A large part of this book is the clinical section, with case studies in which a client, as a grandchild, has either a real or imagined relationship with a grandmother or grandfather. I am grateful that my clients have given their consent for the publication of case histories that have been anonymized. Since the issue involves a multi-generational perspective, the issue of intergenerational transmission of trauma will inevitably be affected and therefore included in the analysis. The therapeutic approach in turn is based on an intersubjective approach as it is currently being discussed among Jungians and psychoanalysts (Chapter 7) and detailed in the case histories (Chapter 8). The book ends with a chapter about the paternal grandfather of C.G. Jung, who had – although unknown to him – a strong influence on him.

It can be assumed that the relationship with the grandparents is subject to change. At the beginning of life they are important and interesting; at some point they lose their meaning, which is not only reflected in surveys in client stories, but also in the fairy tale. (The relationship of a grandchild to a grandparent is given more weight in this book, for the simple reason that more grandchildren than grandparents receive therapy.)

If grandparents played an important and positive role in childhood, they are not necessarily seen by the parents as positive. Frequently, the relationship is described as negative. This is an interesting finding. People seem to be more peaceful, sociable and relaxed when they get to a grandparent's age. This has prompted sociologist Peter Gross (2013) to proclaim the demographic as 'calm, contemplative, peaceful and sustainable societies', partly because life expectancy and the numbers in the ageing population have risen. He is not the only one who speaks of the peace potential of the grandparents' generation and their therapeutic corrective effect on society. If you listen to the client, many would likely agree in the light of their childhood memories.

The theme of the grandparent–grandchild relationship is a first attempt to learn more about this special relationship. Many questions remain unanswered. This theme is rarely mentioned in the scientific literature, though individual aspects are examined, such as the transgenerational transmission of trauma. Otherwise, hardly any literature exists, and this special relationship certainly needs further investigation.

Part I

Theoretical section

Chapter 1

Archetypes concept and emergence theory

The archetypes concept by C.G. Jung

One of the most essential components of the analytical psychology of C.G. Jung is the concept of archetypes. In this chapter the concept of archetypes is described in detail in order to better understand the processes that can occur between grandparents and grandchildren. Jung struggled for a definition of the archetypes throughout his whole life. There are very different and conflicting observations and definitions in his work regarding the concept and the nature of the archetype. One of the results is that today different tendencies in analytical psychology have emerged (for an overview, see Hogenson, 2004a; Knox, 2003; Roesler, 2012a).

Jung's point of view was influenced by different scientific perspectives in the early twentieth century – on the one hand from the philosophy of Plato, Kant, Schopenhauer and Nietzsche, but on the other hand he was also open to the biological approach of Darwin or Lamarck, and later to the physical conceptions of Pauli. Moreover, Jung, as Freud, stands in the tradition of psychiatric Romanticism and the philosophy of nature, according psychiatry and psychology historian Henri F. Ellenberger (Ellenberger, 2011). One has to keep these various influences in mind when it comes to Jung's perspective of the concept of archetypes.

Jung makes a key difference that he maintains in his work: he distinguishes the *archetype* per se from the *archetypal image*. He assigns to the archetype per se an a priori structure, which is inherent to humans of all ages and characterizes our perception possibilities. With the use of the terms 'a priori' and 'per se' the epistemological influence of Kant is proven with the distinction of an unexperienced thing in itself ('natura archetypa') and the phenomena perceived with our senses ('natura ectypa') without Jung having done this intentionally or getting deeply into it. The archetype in itself is abstract and unconscious – and transcendent. Jung writes in 1947 in *On the Nature of the Psyche*: 'it seems to me probable that the real nature of the archetype is not capable of being made conscious, that it is transcendent, on which account I call it psychoid' (Jung, 1947, §417).

On the other hand, he uses scientific analogies from physics and chemistry for the definition of the archetypes. In 1919 he assumed that the archetype is like a form without content, comparing it to a (crystal) structure which has no special features but when in a solution a structure (a crystal) is formed. The specific crystal is different in each case, but the general arrangement of the molecular structure is always the same for all crystals (Jung, 1919, §589, fn 6).

In the much-discussed paper 'Synchronicity: An acausal connecting principle', Jung uses biological analogies: 'The archetypes are formal factors responsible for the organization of unconscious psychic processes; they are "patterns of behaviour"' (Jung, 1952, §841). With this definition Jung moves the archetypes per se into the vicinity of instincts and impulses, referring to animals that also know such archetypal backup-and-response systems:

> There is nothing to prevent us from assuming that certain archetypes exist even in animals, that they are grounded in the peculiarities of the living organism itself and are therefore direct expressions of life whose nature cannot be further explained. Not only are the archetypes, apparently, impressions of ever-repeated typical experiences, but, at the same time, they behave empirically like agents that tend towards the repetition of these same experiences.
>
> (Jung, 1942, §109)

To be exact:

> The instinct of the leaf-cutting ant fulfils the images of ant, tree, leaf, cutting, transport, and the little antgarden of fungi. If any of these conditions is lacking, the instinct does not function, because it cannot exist without its total pattern, without its image. Such an image is an *a priori* type. It is inborn in the ant prior to any activity, for there can be no activity at all unless an instinct of corresponding pattern initiates and makes it possible.
>
> (Jung, 1947, §398)

Jung uses, in this example, instinct and image in the same breath. What the instinct is for animals, the image is for people (whereas Jean Knox (2003) speaks of 'image schema' as we shall see later).

These archetypal backup-and-response systems have been reflected in the collective memory over the centuries: 'The archetype is a kind of readiness to produce over and over again the same or similar mythical ideas' (Jung, 1942, §109). More important than the content of the mythical ideas of the archetypes per se is for Jung the willingness to produce these images. However, it needs certain environmental features in order to start the process. The 'patterns of behaviour' only set up with particular environmental features.

The forces driving this process also have a certain quality that he defines as the numinous ability of archetypes. Again, in *On the Nature of the Psyche* he writes in 1947:

> the archetypes have, when they appear, a distinctly numinous character which can only be described as 'spiritual', if 'magical' is too strong a word.... In its effect it is anything but unambiguous. It can be healing or destructive, but never indifferent, provided of course that it has attained a certain degree of clarity. Often it drives with unexampled passion and remorseless logic towards its goal and draws the subject under its spell, from which despite the most desperate resistance he is unable, and finally no longer even willing, to break free, because the experience brings with it a depth and fullness of meaning that was unthinkable before.
>
> (Jung, 1947, §405)

Just as the instinct is pushing for completion of the action, the archetype pushes to its goal. People experience this as emotional, and numinous.

> For when an archetype appears in a dream, in a fantasy or in life, it always brings with it a certain influence or power by virtue of which it either exercises a numinous or a fascinating effect, or impels to action.
>
> (Jung, 1942, §109)

In Jung's definition of archetypes, we have summarized a combination of perspectives, the world's knowledge aspects (patterns of perception), behavioural aspects (backup-and-response pattern, 'patterns of behaviour'), affective states (numinous feeling, feeling of meaning, fascination) and the definition of an image. This image appears to be more than we commonly understand an image to be; it seems to be more an image representation, or something similar (Hogenson, 2009, p. 328); it seems to have an onto-logical quality; it seems to affect the essence of the thing, the archetype per se.

The image of the leaf-cutting ant is not the same as the archetypal image that Jung distinguishes from the archetype per se. While he finds no definitive definition to the latter, the matter is simpler with the arche-typal images. They differ from the formal archetype per se as they have conscious ability, subjective experience and are influenced by culture and history. They appear in the present world of man in the form of arche-typal ideas, motifs, symbols, image representations, patterns, narratives, relationships or behaviour. They are mediated by the (collective) uncon-scious (Jung, 1947, §417). Everything, whatever we say about arche-types, is illustrations or specific items, which reflect the human perception the behaviour and the affective states. The archetype per se is, as mentioned, unconscious. The archetypal image can therefore be found in narratives as myths and fairy tales, depending on the culture or era, but revolves around the same core. Thus, for example, Heracles', Hiawatha's or Beowulf's archetypal image of the hero archetype emerged, but in different places and in different cultures and time (ancient Greece, the Iroquois tribe USA, Scandinavia).

Current debate of archetypes per se

In the recent debate, Jung's different approaches to the archetypes per se were incorporated and further developed by Jungians: Antony Stevens represents a purely biological understanding of archetypes with his view that they are neuropsychic centres responsible for the coordination of the behavioural and mental repertoire of our species. He localizes them to the genes (Stevens, 1982), and favours therefore a more evolutionary interpretation. According to him and his colleague John Price, archetypes are neuropsychic units caused by evolutionary selection. They are responsible for the behavioural characteristics as well as for the affective and cognitive experiences that are typical of people (Stevens & Price, 1996, p. 6).

In particular, James Hillman takes a very different position by empha-sizing the archetypal psychology, which began with the image, not with the brain physiology or structure of language (Hillmann, 1983, pp. 14ff.). Furthermore, Hillmann tries to recognize and determine the many cultural myths and fantasies that shape the human psyche. He states that we are much more influenced by these archetypal images in the form of personifications of gods, goddesses or other imaginal figures from culture and history (Hillmann, 1983).

A long debate can be observed among Jungians; some favour the opinion that archetypes are more biologically conditioned, others that they are more culturally conditioned. The debate has been intensified recently by representatives of biology and culture who oppose each other (Roesler, 2012b). One possible way out of this reductionist perspective (Martin-Vallas, 2013) is the concept of emergence. But what is meant by this?

Development through emergence theory

Emergence comes from the Latin 'emergere', which means 'allow to appear, emerge'. The biochemist B.H. Weber defines emergence:

> Emergence occurs when new properties appear in a system that were not present in, and could not easily have been predictable from, the properties of the components of the system. Emergent phenomena obey laws that arise with the novel properties. Emergent phenomena impose conditions on their constituents that depend on the nature of the emergent phenomena.
>
> (Weber, 2003, p. 311)

Water is cited as an example; it consists of oxygen and hydrogen. One cannot predict water from this source material. The hydrogen is combined with oxygen in the new phenomenon of water, which has other properties and obeys other laws than its component parts.

The emergence debate was first conducted among scientists in response to reductionist approaches; later, it was picked up in numerous other scientific disciplines, such as developmental psychology, neurobiology and cognition research. In analytical psychology the emergence concept was, among other things, introduced by Treson, Hogenson and Knox (Cambray & Carter, 2004; Hogenson, 2004a; Knox, 2003; Saunders & Skar, 2001; Tresan, 1996). To date, the debate on emergence theory and its relevance to analytical psychology is conducted mainly in English-speaking countries (for an overview, see Bovensiepen, 2011).

In the Jungian discussion, emergence theory is used to try to understand intrapsychic as well as intersubjective processes. Specifically, what needs to be understood is the qualitative, spontaneous and surprising jumps in therapies that lead to a new level, with new laws and new structures, which was not suspected at the start. On the intersubjective level, this refers to surprising transfer/countertransference experiences; on the interpsychic level it is new insights, symbolization or archetypes. Joe Cambray and Linda Carter, two American Jungians, emphasize the feeling of surprise and the dynamizing moment that accompany an emergent process (Cambray & Carter, 2004).

George B. Hogenson argues that the key to understanding the archetypes is to consider them as purely emergent phenomena. He defines archetypes as the emergent property of a dynamic development system of the brain, environment and narrative. In other words, the archetype is a phenomenon that arises in a narrative due to human biology that interacts with the environment (Hogenson, 2004a). Archetypes are then only the product of an emergence process.

This is, of course, a radical position that doesn't remain unchallenged. Antony Stevens and, less strongly, Jean Knox reject this. They argue that with such a position Jung's view of the archetypes per se is no longer necessary. There is no longer a place or a localization, no more an innate neuropsychic potential of the archetype. Stevens argues that Hogenson's definition describes rather an updated phenomenon of archetypes, that is the archetypal image rather than the archetype per se (Stevens, 2003, p. 284).

Jean Knox also expresses criticism, but at the same time formulates a new conceptual framework for the explanation of archetypes, which is also based on the principle of emergence. It refers to the findings of developmental psychologists and cognitive biologists. Johnson and Morton described in 1991 a gene that makes the newborn baby focus on the structures of the human face longer than other structures (Johnson & Morton, 1991, cited in Knox, 2003, pp. 50f.). The structure, which appears very often, is the maternal face (or another important caregiver). Knox argues that this does not mean that this structure possesses an innate symbolic content, but that simple stimulus–response sequences are coming into play. The mother brings communication, too, which activates the child's neural structures and his or her own communication, and so on. This simple activated gene pattern thus has a major impact, because it launches a development sequence that strengthens the attachment and promotes neuronal development. Knox defines this process as the interactions model of human psychological development (Knox, 2003).

Jean Knox, just like Stevens, criticizes that something in Hogenson's definition of archetype is lost, namely the characteristic of the archetype per se. Knox compares it with a primitive sketch or with a Gestalt with no information or representational content (Knox, 2003 p. 64). In addition, innate mechanisms focus the child's attention on features in the environment that are crucial for the infant's survival; these mechanisms have a biological basis and are created by the process of natural selection because they improve the chances of survival. Congenital mechanisms are activated by environmental stimuli, interact with and organize them, resulting in the formation of primitive spatial and conceptual representations (image schemas or archetypes). These build the foundations on which the later more complex representations can be established (Knox, 2003, pp. 61ff.).

These primitive image schemas are more or less universal, they direct the attention of the infants to basic conditions of the environment. They are the same everywhere in the world, and can therefore be described as archetypes per se, as 'image schemas' in the sense of an information-processing model of archetypes per se that internalizes everyday experience and patterns of core meanings (Knox 2003, p. 9). While the abstract pattern itself or image schema can never be experienced directly, it represents an invisible backbone for all the metaphorical characteristics that are expressed in (archetypal) images.

With the concept of image schemas, Knox offers a more development-psychological explanation of archetypes. She even includes in her book *archetypes, attachment* and *analysis* (Knox, 2003) next to developmental psychology epistemological considerations and emergence theory. There is an interaction, according to Knox, between image schema and the environment, in which arises differentiated structures, which run on the principle of emergence. However, she establishes emergent phenomena more strongly as in developmental psychology and learning experiences than does Hogenson.

Jung already mentioned the importance of the environment for the emergence of archetypes, as Martin-Vallas notes (Martin-Vallas, 2013, p. 280), but without knowing the term, by intuitively assessing the environment as important for the emergence of an archetype. We see this in the above example of the leaf-cutter ant, whose instinct does not work, according to Jung, without specific environmental features. Just as every bird can only build a nest in a particular environment, an archetype can only develop in a particular environment. In this sense, an archetype has a more emergent and complex structure as a product of the encounter between environment, caregivers and instinct.

But what does that mean? Aside from physical environmental stimuli such as heat, water or the availability of materials that stimulate the bird to build a nest, or maternal faces that draw the attention of the child, other factors must also play a role. Environmental features alone are not enough for an archetype to occur. It needs additionally a human characteristic that drives the process. The post-Kleinian and Jungian Francesco Bisagni argues for the 'unsaturated innate potential for becoming a subject' (Bisagni, 2009, p. 10). The original self is unsaturated and interacts in the process of deintegration and reintegration dynamically with the object and the environment. The unsaturated expectations are still without content, and only in the interaction process are structures created. Bisagni argues that an infant is born with such unsaturated expectations that must be satisfied in one or another form for it to survive. Such expectations are, in his view, archetypal, with no representative or symbolic content. If the archetype is saturated, a content or a representation exists. (Here, Bisagni argues in terms of object relations theory.) The result of introjections is a sense of self and a centre. The merit of Bisagni is to have introduced the concept of unsaturated archetype as a potential, as an expectation with an a priori structure.

But the question remains: to what extent are these processes biological, and to what extent developmental? Does it need an image schema, a blueprint so to speak, which is genetically fixed, in order to explain archetypes, or is the view of the image schema not exactly an archetypal image and so does not explain the archetype per se (Hogenson, 2004a). Is the image of the unsaturated archetypal expectations an a priori image or genetically determined? Is it the case that an image schema that one can never directly experience is an evolutionary psychological achievement and can be connected with the concept of the archetype per se, as an invisible frame, with which the conscious archetypal images can be expressed (Knox, 2003 p. 62)? Also, questions remain regarding image schemas: what exactly is an image schema? How is it related to time, place and causality? Is Knox's reasoning too developmental? What can we know with our consciousness? Or, in Jung's words,

> it seems to me probable that the real nature of the archetype is not capable of being made conscious, that it is transcendent.... Moreover, every archetype, when represented to the mind, is already conscious and therefore differs to an indeterminable extent from that which caused the representation.
>
> (Jung, 1947, §417)

Pursuant to Hogenson, Knox argues too much from a developmental perspective, since many archetypal images, as described by the Jungian

Donald Kalsched in his clinical experience with patients, cannot be explained by developmental psychology. Kalsched describes in an article the memories of abuse in a patient's childhood (Kalsched, 1996). During the session, she remembers the image of the Virgin Mary, who took the child in her arms and comforted her while she was abused as a real child. This archetypal image appeared then and was more than just an image; it helped her to maintain a sense of self. It was more than its individual parts, but had new characteristics in accordance with emergence theory. Even at the meeting with Kalsched, the power of this archetypal image was still noticeable.

There is another recent example from a daily newspaper that presents the effect of an archetype very beautifully: The article 'Sterbebegleitung für ein Kind' (Terminal care for a child) tells the story of a 7-year-old child who was stricken with cancer. By the time the diagnosis was established, the disease was already well advanced. The parents refused chemotherapy because the chances of survival were minimal. The parents did not want that for their daughter and opted for palliative care. The daughter, Marina, knew she had cancer and would not live much longer. To facilitate the last few months for the whole family, the mother invented the 'herb woman'.

They needed a kind of star to which Marina could orient herself, that could guide her through this difficult time. They needed an ally. And because Marina loved nature, intense fragrances and herbs and flowers, her mother created the figure of the herb woman 'Chrysanthemia'. For Marina it was a woman who lived in the woods, saw everything and could talk to animals. Chrysanthemia was there for all sick children, and comforted them. One day she laid a velvet sack filled with ivy and pine needles at the front door, with a letter along with a power stone in it. Marina's mother told the journalist, when Marina gripped the stone: 'When we saw her face', said she, 'we knew it would work' (Weber, 2013).

The herb woman Chrysanthemia became a part of the family. They searched the woods for her house, for her things that she left in velvet sacks for Marina with suggestions, tea and comforting quotes. Marina took everything without objection, said thanks, drew her into her heart and made drawings, as did her siblings. So the herb woman had become a rock for the entire family. She appeared, stimulated the family and united them around a centre, an archetypal symbol.

Hogenson advocates for such an emergent, ontological approach to understanding the archetypes and their impact (Hogenson, 2004a). In other words, archetypes are the product of an emergent process and depend on the brain, the environment and the narratives that are told in interactions (Hogenson, 2004a, 2009).

Such a view makes perfect sense. The philosopher Roland Barthes achieves a similar result from a completely different perspective.

Roland Barthes' *punctum* and its archetypal effect

Roland Barthes was sorting his photos one November evening after the death of his mother. He was hoping to find an 'appropriate' photo of his mother, 'to find her' for a fleeting moment and 'to recognize' her. He searched the apartment in which she had recently died; under the glow of his mother's lamp the many photos showed him the beloved face. He found it in a picture that showed the mother as a 5-year-old child. In his opinion, he had found the true essence of his mother – and finally found his mother again. Barthes describes the image without reproducing it because the image was too private. Numerous other pictures are published in *Camera Lucida* (Barthes, 2010).

Barthes now defines this moment of 'seeing' as a *punctum*. It reminds him of Proust, who, one day as he bent down to take off his shoes, suddenly discovered the true face of his grandmother in his memory. He felt the same while looking at a photo of his mother, that this 'collected all the possible predicates from my mother's being was constituted and whose suppression or partial alteration, conversely, had sent me back to these photographs of her which had left me so unsatisfied' (Barthes, 2010, p. 70).

In this small text on photography, Roland Barthes distinguishes the *punctum* from *study*. The *study* of the image is a conscious procedure. Suddenly, however, an element of the image could draw awareness, break through the *study*, and pierce the viewer (i.e. an unconscious action).

> A Latin word exists to designate this wound, this prick, this mark made by a pointed instrument; [I call it] *punctum*; for *punctum* is also: sting, speck, cut, little hole – and also a cast of the dice. A photograph's *punctum* is that accident which pricks me (but also bruises me, is poignant to me).
>
> (Barthes, 2010, pp. 26f.)

Another characteristic of the *punctum* is therefore that it affects the viewer, hits him, and the picture thus begins to interest him. It appears in a flash and has then an expansive force. The detail can determine the entire picture. Barthes says that a detail attracts him to a picture; it is just about this detail: 'I feel that its mere presence changes my reading that I am looking at a new photograph, marked in my eyes with a higher value. This "detail" is the *punctum*' (Barthes, 2010, p. 42). Providing details of the *punctum*, it reveals itself. The *study* has to look with a more virtuous attitude. Furthermore, the *punctum* awakes a great kindness, almost emotion. 'Yet, the punctum shows no preference for morality or good taste' (Barthes, 2010, p. 43). It is, so to speak, beyond good and evil and cannot be placed on purpose by the photographer; it is created unintentionally. It 'rings' something in the viewer, triggers a small vibration.

The thus striking detail makes the photograph special; it is no longer just any. The study allows a photograph to be understood immediately; you can give it a label at once: 'What I can name cannot really prick me', says Barthes (Barthes, 2010, p. 51). If I cannot name something, however, it triggers anxiety; you will be tied up, but you do not know why, you cannot locate the action.

> The effect is certain but locatable, it does not find its sign, its name: it is sharp and yet lands in a vague zone of myself; it is acute yet muffled, it cries out in silence. Odd contradiction: a floating flash.
>
> (Barthes, 2010, pp. 52f.)

Sometimes it manifests itself only in retrospect, in the aftermath of the event, something remains of the image, a shoe buckle, a necklace. The memory (the unconscious) appears subsequently without one being able to define – without knowing why – one remembers something from the picture. The *punctum* refers to something completely abstract; it is something 'real', the right degree when opening a hand.

Barthes describes in *Camera Lucida* what happens to him when he finds the *punctum* in a photo. One can assume that he describes perceptive, behavioural and affective patterns that create the archetypes per se. With *punctum*, a numinous, meaningful sense, a depth and centring of perception and behaviour is set, which is also present in an archetypal experience. The conception of Hogenson (2004a) that an ontological and emergent process is taking place is worthy of support. Development psychological processes play an important role in the development of archetypal *images*, however. This will be explained in the next chapter.

Chapter 2

Symbols and analytical psychology

The symbolic concept by C.G. Jung

C.G. Jung had a strong interest in myths, symbols, ethnology and the various world religions since the early twentieth century. In 1910 he read books about excavations in Babylon and a compilation of several volumes entitled *Symbolik und Mythologie der alten Völker* (Symbolism and mythology of ancient people) (Creuzer, 1819–1823). From these readings, the idea for the book on the fantasies of Miss Miller, with the title 'Wandlungen und Symbole der Libido' (*Psychology of the Unconscious*), resulted (Jung, 1925, p. 50; today volume 5 of the *Collected Works* is entitled *Symbols of Transformation*). This is the book that ultimately estranged him from Sigmund Freud and his ideas. Instead of proceeding as a reductionist like Freud, Jung looks at archetypal images and symbols as a creative power and wants to include them in all their width and diverse cultural expressions. Jung sees the symbol as a psychological processing facility that helps to calm the people and to find their centre. Symbols cannot be consciously created; they arise subconsciously because of archetypes, personal experiences, emotions, sensations and within a collective, cultural context. 'The symbols were never devised consciously, but were always produced out of the unconscious by way of revelation or intuition', says Jung (Jung, 1928, §92). With symbols the individual meets with the collective.

Jung wants to decipher the complexity and diversity of the symbol with the question: what is the purpose of the symbol? Therefore, the analytical psychology of C.G. Jung is finally aligned. Jung has a diametrically opposed position to Freud, who is less interested in the symbol per se, but – in a causal way of looking – for what the symbol is hiding. The psyche can be represented symbolically in the approach of analytical psychology in processes such as dreams, fantasies, images, stories and activities, as Verena Kast pointed out in her overview in *The Dynamics of the Symbols* (Kast, 1992).

The term 'symbol' is not distinguished from the 'archetypal image', both of which are translated as allegory. The symbol is an idea, an image that makes sense, loaded with meaning. The symbol thus puts something together (Greek: *symballo* = together); it consists of a material part and a spiritual, non-material part. It contains a surplus of meaning and seems to be, on the one hand, conscious and rational, and on the other hand, unconscious. There is an objectively observable, visible meaning and an invisible, more hidden, irrational significance. This irrational meaning cannot be defined; it is understandable only to those who experience the symbol. Jung defines the concept of symbol in a quote often used as follows. He says the term symbol is 'the best possible description or formulation of a relatively unknown fact, which is … known to exist or is postulated as existing' (Jung, 1916, §148).

While for some persons an image represents a deeper meaning (of a symbol), it has no meaning for someone else. For example, a national flag can represent a powerful symbol to a patriot, but for someone who is at home everywhere in the world and to whom the nation has no meaning, it symbolizes nothing. The national flag itself is only one substantive piece of cloth for him and leaves him cold; for the patriots, however, it is a symbol with an emotional and physical effect.

For Jung, symbols originally had a meaning of expression character and impression character at the same time:

> on one hand, they express the intrapsychic process in images; but, on the other hand, when they have become image, 'incarnated' as it were in a pictorial material, they 'make an impression', that is, their meaning content influences the intrapsychic process and furthers the flow of psychic energy,

as Jolande Jacobi explains, in summing up Jung's life's work (Jacobi, 1973, p. 94). Jacobi mentions the example of a client's withered tree of life that shows pictorially that the latter had lost connection with his naturalistic instincts. Through the awareness of the image, a direction has been shown to him in which he could develop. In fact, in clinical practice this is experienced repeatedly; symbolic images can indicate where the problem is and where the development could proceed. Therefore, Jacobi writes that symbol transformers are mental events (Jacobi, 1973).

Jacobi mentions a second feature of the symbolic image: they are surrounded by personal experiences and deceptive traits of childhood memories. But the deeper you penetrate, the stronger becomes the effect of the symbol; it becomes archetypal:

> for it encloses an archetype, a nucleus of meaning that is not representable in itself but charged with energy. It is very much as when we print an engraving: the first print is extremely sharp, its slightest details are discernible and its meaning is clear; the following prints become poorer in detail and definition; and in the last perceptible image the outlines and details are quite blurred, though we can still distinguish the basic form which leaves all the possible aspects open or combines them.
>
> (Jacobi, 1973, p. 95)

That's how it exists in the child. An example: a child has some repeatedly and similar emotional experiences with his grandmother, and has therefore an inner image of her. This image of the grandmother is enriched by stories and tales and begins in deeper layers to carry archetypal features: the grandmother becomes the old woman or a wicked witch, depending on the experiences gathered. The symbolic image of the real grandmother is reduced on the archaic, collective, subconscious level to the image of an old lady, the witch or even of a dragon.

Current discussion of the symbols in analytical psychology

Symbols and emergence

In the present discussion of symbols, Jungians incorporate neuropsychological, anthropological and developmental arguments. The discussion is mainly dominated by the emergence debate that arose from the mid-1990s (Cambray & Carter, 2004; Hogenson, 2004b; Knox, 2003; Saunders & Skar, 2001; Tresan, 1996). There are different weightings at one end: the Americans George Hogenson, Joe Cambray and Linda Carter have a more ontological perspective; at the other end, the Englishwoman Jean Knox has a more developmental perspective.

Hogenson's view is that the term *emergence* can better describe the depth of a transformation through archetypal symbols, as they occur in dreams or imaginations. The effect of a symbol can be understood with an ontological approach. An example from our own practice describes this situation: a client recounts a dream he had and did not understand: the dream begins in the transit area of an airport building where he initially waits cheerfully. He eventually gets called and starts a long walk through the building until he finally comes to a remote, abandoned part and outside he sees a burnt piece of a jet engine and debris lying around an aeroplane. Asked about associations, he says the evening before he and his wife spoke about his sometimes irascible nature with his young son. In the discussion of the dream he *suddenly* discovers that through his long hours at work he devotes too little time to his family, he invests too little in this part of his life and that his jet engine is actually burnt out. He leaves the meeting surprised, upset and dismayed because he had not seen this himself and says thanks several times for it.

The dream symbolizes his situation. The client seemed shocked and changed. This is what is meant by an emergent process, the appearance of a symbolic image enables awareness and can initiate a new development. (It is to be critically noted that not every symbol is capable of triggering a profound transformation.)

Hogenson further argues that symbolic images have similar features, like phase transitions in thermodynamics. A phase transition, for example, is the transition from a liquid to a solid form, such as when liquid water turns to ice. This is a process that can happen suddenly (Hogenson, 2004b). Hogenson suspects that the nature and function of symbols could be compared with mathematical operations and concepts from biology, chemistry and physics (Hogenson, 2005, p. 278). He refers to the neuroscientist and anthropologist Terrance Deacon from the University of California Berkeley, who wrote numerous articles about nature and function of symbols. Deacon says that symbolic references are not random or arbitrary, as some linguists or cognitive scientists believe:

> [T]here are indeed constraints that are implicit in symbol use. The point I want to emphasize here, however, is that such semiotic constraints as involve symbol systems are located neither in brains nor in society, per se. They are a bit like the formal constraints that have shaped the development of mathematics (and yield such curious universal phenomena as prime numbers).
>
> (Deacon, 2003, p. 98)

Such hypotheses would mean the symbolic world appears when the environmental conditions are such that the appearance is possible. Such an approach is definitely different from the perception of the object relations theorists, for whom symbols present an internal representation. They would mean that symbols function with a relative autonomy within the self-organized area, and that their emergence in accordance to Hogenson could possibly be explained by mathematical laws.

The relative autonomy of the symbols is also emphasized by the two American Jungians, Joe Cambray and Linda Carter. On the basis of their emergence theories, they see symbols as mediators between the unconscious and consciousness:

> They are formed as composite products from encounters with affectively charged mental states, saturated with activated unconscious material: ... they are the psychological instantiation of the emergent 'third' of the interactive field (whether intrapsychic or interpersonal) in those moments when the field is poised at the edge of chaos and order, the locus for the origins of life itself.
>
> (Cambray & Carter, 2004, p. 121)

Elements or structures suddenly appear there, and can be positive or negative and are accompanied by a feeling of surprise and a stimulating feeling (Cambray, 2010). Cambray and Carter assume that even archetypal patterns showed in myths, fairy tales and general narratives have emergent properties. The interactive network of this archetypal pattern serves as a node or focal point (Cambray & Carter, 2004, p. 119).

However, Hogenson, Cambray and Carter do not reject the importance of developing psychological insights for the development of symbols in the individual, as the Jungian Jean Knox writes, but they do not put so much weight on it.

Symbols and image schema

Jean Knox includes research results of attachment theory and cognitive and neuropsychological research in her consideration of the emergence of the psychic. At an early age a child begins to compare and sort the information he or she collects, which forms the base of the symbolization process (Knox, 2003).

Symbolic meaning is not genetically anchored information. That is not possible, because meaning can change historically and culturally. What represented the ideal beauty in the baroque era no longer applies in the twenty-first century. There are an infinite number of different symbolic images and symbolic meanings. This depends on the particular culture, from their collectively formed narrative and story types, which are passed on culturally and through social interactions. The child has experiences with the grandmother or the grandfather and hears stories about grandparents or older figures in fairy tales, stories, fables, legends and myths. This creates an inner symbolic concept about grandparents. Children automatically give these stories meaning; they categorize them in a certain way. If certain experiences are repeated again and again, the results according to the Jungian Gustav Bovensiepen (2011) are certain internal working models with patterns of meaning, affective tones and expectations.

Jean Knox argued in more detail how these patterns of meaning emerge. She explains in her often-cited book *Archetype, Attachment, Analysis: Jungian Psychology and the Emergent Mind* (Knox 2003) that symbolic images are constructed around an 'image schema'. This happens, according to Karmiloff-Smith (1992), through the process of an internal rewriting, and according to Fordham (1985) through the process of deintegration and reintegration of information. Again and again a quantity of new information is absorbed through the senses and compared with the patterns of core meanings that are slowly built up in the psyche, which could be described as 'inner working models' of personal identity and relationships, as proposed by John Bowlby (1973). Such a model is obvious, because repeated experiences form internalized patterns. We have to somehow arrange or interpret the sensations. This forms symbolic experiences with emotional connotations.

An example: when I asked 'What was your experience with your grandmother?', a client replied: 'She was a witch!' I said nothing, surprised – as was the client. The word came up suddenly; we had not talked before about witches or similar figures. I asked what she meant. She said she did not know; the word simply came to her mind. She says, after a pause, her paternal grandmother was actually fine with her, not very nice, but also not mean or cold. But with her mother she was unfair, nasty and derogatory, and sometimes did not speak with the father for weeks. The client had taken a symbol to express an experience that she had not made by herself, but one of her parents – and it shows her unconscious identification with them.

According to Jean Knox, this symbol formation can be explained by the emergence of a witch's 'image schemas', caused by narratives and internal working models and the parents' patterns of meaning. This leads the child to develop similar symbol patterns or archetypal images.

According to attachment theory, the patterns of meaning from the parents are important for the emergence of such patterns in children (Knox, 2003, p. 207).

A child encounters various narratives in his biography, stories or fairy tales that are told to him to fall asleep, mythological films that he sees, real stories that he hears. All this can also be superimposed, for example, when a storyteller tells a story and includes his own thoughts and feelings. That does not have to happen consciously. It can be thoughts and feelings of the storyteller from his biography, and the child absorbs it. According to the interpersonal neurobiologist D.J. Siegel (2012), the storyteller and listeners produce a discourse together. Stories, according to him, have an organizing function and enable integration, as we saw in the first chapter with respect to the herbalist. Siegel argues:

> In the co-construction of stories, parent and child enter into a dyadic form of a bilateral resonance. Each person enters a state of interhemispheric integration, which is facilitated by interpersonal communication.... This highly complex form of collaborative communication allows the dyad to move into highly resonant states, and also enables the child's mind to develop its own capacity for integration. Such a capacity may be at the heart of self-regulation.
>
> (Siegel, 2012, p. 374)

Applied to our subject, it can be summarized that early experiences with grandparents can lead to symbolic patterns; according to Knox, so-called image schemas are built up. Ontologically considered, as proposed by Hogenson, an archetype is activated depending on the environment of experiences with grandparents. Children experience grandparents as meaningful persons and these experiences can be stored as meaningful in implicit memory, next to other experiences.

By this, in a psyche different part-psyches arise (Bovensiepen, 2006), which do not have to be linked. Each contains its own feelings, perceptions, expectations, fantasies, defences, memories and mental representations, as we shall see in Chapter 4.

Chapter 3

Images of age in narratives (fairy tales, myths, stories and legends)

As mentioned in the previous chapter, a child hears different narratives during their childhood; stories are told as they fall asleep, fairy tales in kindergarten, filmed stories that are watched at home. Some stories are told by the child's caregivers, others by the media. In these narratives, the elderly play a prominent role and can arouse in the child feelings and different expectations of dealing with older people, especially with grandparents. Grandparents do not even have to be personally known, but because every child has grandparents they are important in the same way as parents.

A cognitive psychologist and researcher on the concept of mental representations, Anthony J. Marcel, emphasizes our need for representations of the past – narratives – to help with our current actions. Otherwise we would be very dependent on the present circumstances, and couldn't compare our actions with previous ones (Marcel, 1988).

From the previous chapters it has become clear that narratives and archetypal images in the narratives can mark us. In this chapter, therefore, we are interested in the descriptions of the elderly, which is why we want to present these narratives in detail. Of interest is the question of how the relationship between the elderly and a child looks, how this evolves, what is offered, which implicit rules exist and how a child or young person responds. If it turns out that the same pattern is always described, we can speak of generalized expectations in dealing with older persons which can be stored in the implicit or explicit memory, as Karmiloff-Smith suggested from a cognitive perspective (Karmiloff-Smith, 1992).

Knox uses the term *image schema*, something by which incoming information can be organized and categorized in the memory (Knox, 2003, p. 64). This term refers to the relationship patterns in narratives: hypothetically it can be said that the existing narratives regarding grandparents revolve around four image schemas or archetypes: the 'old wise man', the 'the old wise woman', the 'evil wizard' and the 'witch'. However, further studies are necessary in order to consolidate this hypothesis.

Jean Knox also uses Bowlby's concept of the 'internal working model' (Bowlby, 1969). Relationship patterns are visible in the internal working model, which can affect the perception and behaviour of a child with respect to present people. The internal working models are not necessarily conscious; they are even more unconscious or implicit. They can be passed down through generations. Parents and grandparents have heard stories, fairy tales, legends and tales of the elderly, and they tell them to their children in a certain way.

Below, we will focus on symbolic figures and relationship patterns in these four image schemas in narratives, with the hypothesis that the resulting internal working models can influence the relationships of grandparents and children.

Positive narratives of male images of age

The positive narratives about older men are examined as they are formed over the centuries and how they occur repeatedly in myths, legends, stories and fairy tales in sometimes very different cultures. Whereas combat, adventure, love and passion are the great themes of the stories of heroes and heroines, those passions in stories of old men are less available – they are more likely to be found outside of such subjects (Moore & Gillette, 1991). How are the elderly and their relationship patterns to young people characterized?

C.G. Jung and the old wise man 'Philemon'

For C.G. Jung, the figure of the wise old man played a prominent role, so it shall be briefly discussed. He described the shape of the old man in 'The Phenomenology of the Spirit in Fairytales' (1945) and in 'Aion. Researches into the Phenomenology of the Self' (1950). He called him the 'wise old man' and described him as follows: 'The wise old man appears in dreams in the guise of a magician, doctor, priest, teacher, professor, grandfather, or any other person possessing authority' (Jung, 1945, §398). The wise old man is characterized on the one hand as someone with knowledge, insight, reflection, wisdom and intuition, and on the other hand as one with moral qualities such as benevolence and helpfulness (Jung, 1945, §406).

After 1912 Jung had a profound experience with an inner figure, which he called 'Philemon' and with whom he maintained an intimate relationship over the years. Philemon was a gaunt old man with white hair, a white beard and wings; he dressed in something like a priest's robe. Jung held inner dialogues with him when a major crisis emerged after termination of his professional positions and his separation from the ideas and person of Sigmund Freud. The impression of this figure was so strong that he painted it (e.g. in the 'Red Book') and found his path by dialogues with Philemon (Jung, 2009). He looked at Philemon as his inner teacher. (Was Philemon a substitute for Freud? In the painted pictures Philemon and Freud look very similar.) But why Philemon?

Philemon is portrayed in 'Ovid's Metamorphoses' as an old, truly loving, self-sufficient and unselfish man, since he offered food to the unfamiliar gods Zeus and Hermes, although he himself had little (Holzberg, 2007). He is an example of a humble man who rests satisfied in itself. He is related to Baucis, his wife; they have aged together in cheerful equanimity, despite their poverty. The inner figure of Philemon taught Jung to endure contradictions and tensions that emerged when oscillating between love and guilt. Philemon warned him of the soul figure (the anima) and said that he should not be influenced too much by her – she is a woman who wanted to be kept amused. Philemon in Ovid and Philemon by Jung are wise old men that are not affected by passions; they have attained a certain serenity and calmness. These properties correspond to the archetypal image of the wise old man, which is present in many narratives.

The archetypal image of the wise old man

The archetypal image of the wise old man shows up in fairy tales, legends and epics in different but similar forms: He is described as a little old man with a long, grey beard, as in the Estonian fairy tale 'How an Orphan Boy Unexpectedly Found his Luck'. In the story the old man nourishes a boy who had run away, and he gives him advice, his haversack and a little barrel in which he always finds food and drink (Jung, 1945, §§401ff.). Another story describes him as a little wrinkled old man with a green beard, who lives in a green lodge (Jung, 1945, §406); in another he is simply God himself, who shows up as a little man with a long grey beard to repair the damage caused by the devil (Jung, 1945, §412).

In cultural history a series of such old men exist, from the Middle Ages up to the present time, and they are described as wise. There are prophets such as Moses and the Hopi Indian White Feather, the Germanic god Baldur, the Greek god Apollo Hekatos or the sorcerer Merlin, as well as politicians such as Gandhi. (The list goes on and on, especially when characters from novels and fantasy literature are included such as Gandalf in *Lord of the Rings*, Dumbledore in *Harry Potter* or Master Yoda in the movie *Star Wars*.) Sometimes they are referred to simply as 'wise old men' without any further attribution. Even our God image is dominated by the image of the wise old man. We imagine God not as young, but old, equipped with knowledge, experience and wisdom.

A common characteristic of these wise old men is that they live withdrawn from society and are known for their knowledge and wisdom, pass on their advice and assistance to visitors willingly and sometimes have magical or mystical powers – or at least it seems so to those seeking advice. Often the old man seems a little unworldly, unfamiliar or he lives in his own time and world. He seems to place little value on his appearance and appears to be poor. But some wise old men pull, unnoticed in their seclusion, the threads of the story and help the hero to reach his goal.

Let us turn now to the wise old men in the legends of the Middle Ages. This image of the wise old men dominates our perception even today. In the first instance, we refer to Merlin.

Merlin is described as a Welsh wizard in the Arthurian legends that arose for the first time in the twelfth century. His name appears in a number of stories that have a scope spanning France, the UK and Ireland. In a version from 1804 by Dorothea and Friedrich Schlegel (Schlegel, 1804), Merlin is the son of the devil and a God-fearing virgin, making him demi-human. Early on he saves his mother from certain death using his skill with prophecies and surprises those around him again and again with his wisdom. He is appointed as adviser to King Uther Pendragon through his prophetic gifts and proposes him, among other things, to produce a Round Table for his knights for the meetings. A chair should remain empty, for the future King of the Knights of the Round Table. No one but Merlin knows who will be the king. He initiates furthermore the quest for the Holy Grail. Merlin arranges it so he becomes the adviser of Arthur. All of these things happen to protect the kingdom. Also, Merlin decides that only those who could be Uther Pendragon's successor could draw the sword Excalibur from the stone (Merlin had inserted the sword into the stone using magic). As Arthur manages to withdraw the sword, he is known by Merlin as the true king's son and is proclaimed king. Merlin helps Arthur in the subsequent chaos.

Merlin advises Arthur not to be afraid of his enemies, for he will help him. Merlin gives Arthur different advice on how to destroy his enemies and how to bring back the knights to the Round Table. Then Merlin hands him a flag with a bronze dragon that spews bright fire, with an immensely long and thick tail that winds in many curves. Nobody knows where Merlin obtained this flag (Schlegel, 1804, chapter 34).

The relationship between Merlin and Arthur seems to be very intimate; Merlin gives Arthur absolute protection and assistance, a kind of unconditional loyalty that Arthur accepts humbly. The relationship is pure and of great power. This can be seen symbolically in the picture of the bronze dragon on the flag, and in the bright fire. This bond between the old wise man and the young king seems to have an archetypal quality. You could call the handing over of the flag an archetypal moment of meeting. Arthur has been enthroned only recently and is still full of self-doubt, because he was raised and trained as a stable boy, and does not know for certain himself that he is the true king's son. Merlin believes in him, appeals to his royal soul and encourages him.

The function of this old wise man is clear: Merlin is a person that gives a target to the individual and is able to simultaneously bond different fighting groups together. He looks further ahead than others and has the tools needed to overcome discord, strife and hopelessness, such as using Excalibur to make Arthur the king. He is an intermediary who advises the young hero and brings him closer to values such as purity, uniformity and courage. Merlin is also an old wanderer; the fate of the humans is at his heart, and he protects and supports them on their way.

The effects of such representations on the child's psyche regarding inner expectations and patterns of meaning, and generally internal working models, will be described below.

In a diluted form in medieval epics there are many descriptions of such old wise men, such as in the story of *Tristan und Isolde*. In this famous epic (Bédier, 1945), the story of a love triangle between the hero, Tristan, King Marke and Isolde is told. Tristan drinks a love potion that was meant for King Marke and Isolde. Isolde also drinks it, whereupon the two fall madly in love with each other. They have to flee and stay in the deep forest for a while. The two lovers wonder what to do. Isolde suggests seeking the hermit Ogrin, who lives in the forest. He sits on the threshold of his cottage, reading a book. Ogrin knows what happened and confronts them with their love, which brings only misery; he invites them to repent. The hermit is here in the service of the Christian God, who wants penance. Tristan asks for help. He would like to offer peace to the king and is willing to let Isolde go. He himself will travel to Brittany, and if one day the king wants him to come back, he would do so. But Isolde is not willing to repent. Ogrin is nevertheless satisfied and grants them generous help, even knowing that there is a reward for Tristan's head and that Tristan does not regret his sins; Ogrin does not condemn him. He writes a letter to the king with Tristan's offer, in which he also lies to protect them both and to help them get back into the normal world.

Ogrin was probably once a priest who has taken seriously the poverty commandment of the Church, but instead of insisting on remorse and repentance he is touched by the suffering of both. He wants to offer help for reconciliation and is ready to lie. He does not stand for an abstract principle of guilt and atonement, but shows a compassionate heart.

Ogrin and the Hermit 'Trevrizent' in Wolfram's *Parzival* (von Eschenbach, 2003) live alone as ascetics in the solitude of the forest, feeding on herbs and roots. They seem to be needy, poor and dirty; they generally place less emphasis on mundane needs than do others. There are, as Merlin, not monks or priests, but old wise men that live by Christian values and give people advice on how they can be absolved of their sins by Christian acts of charity. Also, Trevrizent draws attention in the epic *Parzival* to fidelity and charity, and to trust in God, which makes someone a knight. In this respect these old wise men are moral authorities and examine the hero for his good heart. If this is the case, then they appear when it is necessary, and can guide the hero to ask the right questions and take a risk.

One may wonder why wise old men are often described as hermits. The educationalist and religious teacher Otto Betz presumed hermits live on the edge of the world in deep forests or mountains because they have dispensed with glory and honour, power and wealth. They stand on the threshold between two worlds; they are patient and loving, and aim at the heart of the matter. Therefore, they are often the one who brings out the true person in the hero. Also, they are the ancestors who pass on secret knowledge (Betz, 2000, p. 277).

Another example of such an archetypal image of an old wise man is Gandalf in the *Lord of the Rings* trilogy (Tolkien, 1991). Merlin is undeniably present in Gandalf's description; Tolkien was no doubt influenced by Merlin. Like Merlin, Gandalf is only partially human; he has more than one life – he dies in the story and reappears later on. He, too, has a big heart and wants to re-establish justice. He also looks for and finds the hero with the pure heart, a hero who is loyal and true and can surpass himself in dangerous situations. He helps the hero and his

associates on their paths; he himself is only a wanderer with old knowledge, instincts and feelings of justice. His heart beats for the small,
unsuspecting and innocent people who suffer for the intrigues of others.
He suffers with and helps them. As Gandalf appears for the first time,
enthroned on a two-wheeled cart in the village, his appearance is
described as follows:

> An old man was driving it all alone. He wore a tall, pointed blue hat,
> a long gray coat, and a silver scarf. He had a long white beard and
> bushy eyebrows that stuck out beyond the brim of his hat.
>
> (Tolkien, 1991, p. 32)

He is known in the village as a firework artist, but his real business is
much more mysterious and dangerous. He is older than anyone thought,
more than 1,000 years old, but he has aged very slowly. He and Frodo's
friend Sam help Frodo, the hero, in the dark land of Mordor, where self-
doubt, fear and terror reign, where depression and emptiness spread and
want to devour and destroy everything. They help to keep him on his
task. In Jungian terms, Gandalf supports the hero to confront and manage
his shadow on his individuation path.

The philologist and fairy tale specialist Maria Christa Maennersdoerfer considers that the figure of the old, despite many details, is only
described vaguely. The nature of the figure remains elusive. Old wise
men occur only occasionally and sparingly within the drama of a story or
fairy tale. Nevertheless, there is the feeling that they are permanently
present, as if they pull invisibly at the strings (Maennersdoerfer, 2000,
p. 150). He encourages the hero to go on, and he arrives unbidden when
the hero needs him, wherever it may come, and from whichever tempo-
rality whatsoever (Maennersdoerfer, 2000, p. 151). His precognition
arises from the edge of the story, because there could probably be no
wisdom without distance from the events.

In the view of Jungian psychologists, the old wise men stand with one
leg outside reality; they have a greater awareness than the person seeking
advice, and may therefore be able to give wise advice. They occur in
transitional periods in where the individual is confused and insecure and
does not know how to proceed.

The previously mentioned narratives describe old wise men as people
who have no dark side, possess magical powers, represent a moral
authority and encourage the young hero to progress. Mostly they live far
away from the community and are only half-human. The narratives

always represent the same relationship patterns, which is why one can speak of generalized relationship patterns.

What impact might such representations have on the child's psyche regarding expectations and patterns of meaning, generally internal working models? With the numerous similar narratives, from a developmental perspective this figure could become an internal working model of the child, which transcends the instance of the parent and helps to stabilize the child who is in a crisis. This internal working model can be applied to a real grandfather. The grandfather is actually 'behind' or 'above' the parents and expands the child's relationship with respect to belonging and tribal consciousness. Grandparents are the 'great parents', the parents of the parents. Their age and possible power is often beyond children's imagination. From an ontological perspective the emergence of the old wise man may suggest that the story is driven in a different direction. The protagonist is able to develop with the magical power of the wise old man, which may also influence an internal working model of a child.

Positive narratives of female images of age

Old women are described in fairy tales, legends and myths as the 'grandmother'; for example, in the Icelandic creation myth *Edda*, or in the fairy tale *The Devil with the Three Golden Hairs*, or as a very old mother in the fairy tale *The Goose Girl at the Well*, or as the old woman with the white hair in the fairytale *The Nixie in the Mill-Pond*. The most famous portrayal of such a woman is in the fairy tale *Mother Holle*. Let's begin with *The Goose Girl at the Well*.

The archetypal image of the old wise woman

In *The Goose Girl at the Well* a very old woman asks a young, carefree Count's son if he'll help her carry her basket of apples, pears and freshly cut grass, to which he agrees willingly (Grimm, 2014, no. 89). But the going proves to be arduous, as well as the route, which is an hour-long march over hill and dale. The apples, pears and grass are getting heavier and heavier; worse still, even the old lady hops up on the basket. The Count's son totters on the path to her house high up in the mountains, where he can recover in a paradisiacal landscape with a clear brook, cackling geese and thousands of flowers and wild thyme. Here, he meets a big, old and ugly 'Trulle' – the goose girl. The old lady hopes that he doesn't fall in love with her, which surprises him. In this place, the world is upside down. A paradisiacal state high up in the mountains! An ugly old woman with whom one might fall in love! No wonder the Count's son wanders in the forest for a long time until he finds his way out again – symbolically speaking, until he finds his way back from this wonderful, unconscious place to the conscious world. The old woman in this fairy tale can work wonders by transforming tears into pearls and a house into a castle. She is friendly, helpful and knows apparently everything that happens in the world. People tend to avoid contact with her as she seems a bit strange. They have a healthy respect for her, unconsciously knowing that one cannot be entirely at ease when dealing with her as she may hijack you into another world. Those who do, however, are richly rewarded – as is the Count's son, who gets the princess, luck, pearls and a castle at the end.

How does the relationship pattern of the two people now look? The young man looks on the one hand naive, and on the other helpful and willing to follow the old woman. The old woman has magical power; she is outside of space and time and indicates ambivalences and contradictions: what is ugly can be beautiful as well, what seems easy can be difficult, etc. She encourages him to endure the contradictions, to grow from a child into an adult.

In the fairy tale *Mother Holle* the magical world is present (Grimm, 2014, no. 24). In this fairy tale, a world by other laws is described; the bread and the tree can talk. Into this world a girl is coming whose attachment needs are not met by a rough and ignoring stepmother. The tree calls the girl:

'Oh, shake me, shake me! We apples are all ripe.' So she shook the tree till the apples fell like rain, and went on shaking till they were all down, and when she had gathered them into a heap, she went on her way. At last she came to a little house, out of which an old woman peeped; but she had such larch teeth the girl was frightened, and was about to run.

(Grimm, 2014, p. 95)

The woman has big teeth – symbolically, she can bite or threaten someone. But she speaks to the girl:

'What are you afraid of, dear child? Stay with me; if you will do all the work in the house properly you will be the better for it. Only you must take care to make my bed well, and shake it thoroughly till the feathers fly – for then there is snow on the earth. I am Mother Holle.' As the old woman spoke so kindly, the girl took courage and agreed to enter her service.

(Grimm, 2014, p. 95)

For the first time the needs of unmet expectations seem to be met. The old woman says: 'Dear child', and 'Stay with me'. This is inviting and must be a new experience for the girl, because her stepmother is hard and repels her. The girl comes into a paradisiacal land where bread and fruits are ripe and ready to be harvested and eaten. Food is available in abundance. Every day there is roast and boiled meat. The world seems warm and flourishing, compared with the cold and heartless world of the stepmother. Therefore, she readily enters into service and performs all tasks. Life here is good; Mother Holle never speaks a harsh word.

The Jungian analyst Ingrid Riedel says that the girl finally grows at the right time from the symbiosis with this archetypal mother (Riedel, 2006). After a while the child gets homesick and wants to go home. Mother Holle meets the child's desire and leads her to a gate. When the gate opens and the girl stands below, there falls a huge shower of gold, and it all remains hanging on her, so that it covers her all over. 'Because you were so busy', says Mother Holle. The girl receives her blessing in the form of gold.

When her lazy sister sees the gold, she wants to experience the same and lets herself fall into the well. She is not afraid when faced with the great teeth of Mother Holle; she has no respect for the laws of the other world; she does not follow her orders; she does not shake the trees, or even the bed of Mother Holle, but only pretends to do so. So Mother Holle soon announces that she has missed her chance. The lazy sister is showered with pitch. She has not opened herself to the archetypal experience, so she has missed the possibilities of this world.

In the relationship of the girl and Mother Holle, the girl's needs have been met. The experience of being showered with gold appears to have a numinous quality with emergent properties. It turns upside down the previous knowledge and the perception of the girl. The old woman is described as powerful and makes a correction of the previous attachment experience possible. The lazy girl could not open up to this archetypal world of the powerful old one; she resists and therefore she is punished.

The grandmother and the young man in The Devil with the Three Golden Hairs

In the fairy tale *The Devil with the Three Golden Hairs* (Grimm, 2014, no. 29) a young boy gets involved with the grandmother of the devil to obtain wisdom that he needs to get the king's daughter to marry him. Verena Kast (1985) interpreted the whole fairy tale, but that is beyond the scope here. I refer to this interpretation but we concentrate on the relationship of the young with the grandmother, who in this fairy tale is a powerful ancient goddess.

The young man needs three golden hairs of the devil to be able to marry. He finds the entrance to Hell, which is black and sooty within, but the devil is not at home. However, his grandmother is sitting in a large armchair. ' "What do you want?" said she to him, but she did not look so very wicked. "I should like to have three golden hairs from the devil's head", answered he, "else I cannot keep my wife"' (Grimm, 2014, p. 110). The young man adds boldly and fearlessly that he also wants to solve three puzzles that have been given to him. The three golden hairs here probably symbolize special cognition and indestructible wisdom.

The sooty hell does not seem to frighten him; his confidence is undiminished. That is a tall order, the grandmother says thoughtfully, 'if the devil comes home and finds you, it will cost you your life'. It seems she is willing to help him; she has empathy with him, which seems strange. Hell is finally the place where nothing else exists but a devil who swallows humans. In this fairy tale, the devil is called a man-eater and, as we see later, is criticized by his grandmother as he always has a nose only for human flesh – he should not overdo it so. It is therefore perhaps better to understand why she worries and why she begins to interfere. Symbolically considered, the grandmother is worried that the world has become devastating. The young man wants to take a wife, but this is denied by the devil, the shadow of the king.

The grandmother turns him into an ant. 'Creep into my folds of my dress, you will be safe there', she says. He must be confident and give up temporarily his shape if he wants to have access to her secret power. The boy must completely abandon his safe world; his perception changes suddenly and he becomes as small as an ant. He can do nothing but listen, since larger forces are in power.

As the evening comes on, the devil returns home. As soon as he enters he notices that the air is not pure. He smells human flesh, he says – this is not right here. He looks into every corner, and searches, but cannot find anything. The grandmother scolds him: 'It has just been swept, and everything is put in order, and now you are upsetting it again; you have always got man's flesh in your nose. Sit down and eat your supper'. After a meal he is mild, and the grandmother puts his head in her lap and says she shall louse him a little. Soon he falls asleep and snores. The old woman grabs a golden hair, tears it out and lays it beside him. The devil cries out and asks what she is doing.

Let us pause: the devil smells the youth but cannot find him. The grandmother scolds him and distracts him from the smell. She does not lie directly, but almost. The devil calms down after eating. The relationship between the two is described as very close and trusting.

The devil puts his head in her lap because he wants to be deloused, as monkeys do with each other. The grandmother wants to come close to the wisdom of the devil and quite rudely rips a hair out. She betrays him, according to the Munich Jungian Joanne Wieland-Burston (Wieland-Burston, 2010, p. 46). One might also assume that she betrays the devil to protect the life that is represented by the young man.

The grandmother answers that she did it in a bad dream. The devil asks her what kind of dream: 'I dreamt that in a certain kingdom there stood an apple-tree which had once borne golden apples, but now would not even bear leaves. What, think you, was the reason?' And the devil answers this riddle. It is interesting that the grandmother begins to lie boldly and the devil doesn't realize. We realize who has the real power in Hell.

Nevertheless, the story is located in a topsy-turvy world in which much isn't in its normal place. The ant is – although protected – close to the devil's head; the grandmother deceives the almighty devil, in Hell, where people are eaten. This is probably an experience that is typical in archetypal situations, where familiar knowledge is no longer valid, and anything can be quite different; you suddenly find yourself in another form, while a figure like the devil is treated as a little boy.

Only the grandmother knows what to do and has access to both worlds, the human and the archetypal world, to the good and bad, the right and wrong. One might also assume she stands at the edge of life and eternity, and does not allow the threat of the dead world of the devil to increase.

Later, she grabs again and pulls out two more hairs and receives answers to two more questions, so that the young man can solve all the puzzles, bring the king the three golden hairs and marry the king's daughter.

The king has mercilessly put task to task to the young man, pursued and tried to kill him. The young man could finally defeat the king with the help of the grandmother – the first and third generations can defeat the middle generation. The grandmother is in better contact with the unconscious and with the secret knowledge, and therefore stronger than the king, whose awareness has become limited. In this perspective the devil is the archetypal variant of the angry king who wants to destroy and annihilate everything new. In this respect, both represent the death principle; the grandmother is the Eros principle, capable of enduring contradictions.

An emergent process is noted because the boy's perception and thinking changes. A co-construction is also observable, as the youth does not passively awaits his fate, but actively demands it. The boy receives in this process what he needs to become a man.

In summary: in narratives with old women it is shown that the old woman is helpful and wise. Jungian analysts such as Verena Kast (1985), Ingrid Riedel (1995) and Marie-Louise von Franz (1977) speak of the archetype of the old wise woman. They have a profound knowledge and offer their magical powers selflessly to the young heroes and heroines. They seem to be more independent and more powerful than their parents, and live away at a border reality, sometimes not even in this reality. Young people fall into this luminal experience, in an ontological and emergent process from which they come back to life in a changed way. In this respect, these narratives describe a generalized relationship pattern.

From a developmental perspective one could say these numerous narratives reflect a basic structure of the archetypal image of the old wise woman, and could lead to an internal working model of the child. The image of the old wise woman could support the self-experience of a child in times of crisis and transition; the grandmother comes to mind because she actually is 'behind' or 'above' the parents, and belongs to the family and to the tribal consciousness, the same as the grandfather.

Negative narratives of male images of age

This chapter is about negative images of old men in narratives like fairy tales, myths and legends, to find out what internal working models could result in such stories for children and adults and what the described relationship pattern looks like.

This refers to stories of destructive old magicians, of evil giant as the 'Rübezahl', trolls, gnomes and dragons. For reasons of space I concentrate here on human beings and their relationship with young people, and focus less on giant, trolls, gnomes and dragons.

We find old evil wizards often in fairy tales, such as in *The Old Wizard and his Children* or the fairy tale *Caliph Stork* by Wilhelm Hauff or in the Grimms' tales *Fitchers Bird* or *Puss in Boots*. Even in fiction or fantasy films, the figure of the evil old magician is well represented. In Tolkien's *Lord of the Rings* he is Saruman, the evil magician opponent of Gandalf. In J.K. Rowling's *Harry Potter* it is Lord Voldemort. This list could be extended arbitrarily.

The archetypal image of the evil wizard

Let us take a typical example of an evil wizard in the Grimm fairy tale *Puss in Boots* (Grimm, 2014, no. 46). A poor miller's son inherits from his father only the cat and wants to make with the last of his money a few warm gloves from her coat. The cat hears this and intervenes; it says he should rather make it a pair of shoes, and then he would see. The cat takes off with the shoes and brings him gold piece after gold piece, as it is sophisticated and can meet the needs of the king. But the cat wants more, namely to marry the poor miller's son to the princess, but for this he must retrieve the country taken by an evil wizard. The meeting of the cat and magician is described as follows:

> He soon comes to the wizard's palace, and goes in boldly. The magician looks at him contemptuously, and asks him what he wants. The cat bows deeply and says that he has heard that the wizard can transform himself into any animal that he wishes – a dog, fox or wolf. But an elephant seems quite impossible, and therefore he comes to see to admire it.

The hero, here in the shape of a cat, provokes and flatters the magician's ego and magical abilities. (Wizards are regularly provoked in fairy tales and do not see the cunning behind it.) The magician in *Puss in Boots* turns proudly into an elephant, but the cat is unimpressed and encourages the wizard to continue by saying that surely he cannot transform himself into a mouse – this is impossible! The magician responds to the flattery, saying 'oh, yes, dear kitten, I can too'. And he jumps around the room as a mouse.

The wizard is so naive and foolish that he does not realize the cat has duped him. You can guess the end. The cat takes the mouse and eats it.

This pattern is present in numerous fairy tales. Sometimes the hero or heroine must operate magical power that means, symbolically speaking, to activate unconscious forces. Marie-Louise von Franz noted the example of such a lengthy struggle in the Russian fairy tale *The Dark Wizard Tsar* (von Franz, 1991, pp. 257ff.).

Destructiveness and megalomania of the evil wizard

The dark wizard tsar has a daughter that he does not want to give to anyone and would prefer to keep. The impossible task he gives to young suitors is to hide, without being able to be found. The young men always fail because the dark wizard has a spellbook in which everything is written. Finally, a young man arrives and attempts the challenge, but he wants three attempts. It turns out that the young man wants to get to know the abilities of the tsar first in order to dupe him.

It is not enough that he turns into fish, birds, wolf or a blade of grass, and also uses magical powers. Only when he makes use of the magical powers of the magic bird Magovej, and the bird undetected brings the intruder back to the castle, does he remain untraceable. The tsar no longer finds him in the spellbook and has to give him his daughter and the throne after his death.

Simple transformation is not enough to break the magical power of the magician. The young man must use the magic of the bird and give up his ego completely, which is an archetypal experience. The evil can only be fought with magic – that means with the instinctive, irrational, creative part of a personality – in order to resist the devastating attacks of the magician.

Of interest is the reaction of the magician when he no longer finds the youth: he seeks him in the nest of the magic bird Magovej, but there he is no longer (the magician cannot keep track of the bird). When he does not find him, he chops everything to pieces, starts a fire and burns everything. He rummages around the earth until nothing is left of the tree, so furious is he – this is the character of a destructive magician. He is limitless in his destructive power and destroys everything that gets in his way. Something remains amid the destruction: the 'treasure' of the wizard, a daughter or a virgin who has to be rescued by the hero.

In 'The phenomenology of the spirit in fairytales' C.G. Jung mentioned the example of a Balkan tale in which an old man in the form of an evil spirit robbed the king's sister. The younger brother of the king finds the spirit, which has now become a dragon, and kills it. A youth springs out of it and marries the sister. The evil spirit had bewitched a whole town, made everyone immovable, rigid (Jung, 1945, §417). In this context Jung speaks of obsession. He mentions another feature: 'the old man acts the part of the villain' (Jung, 1945, §415). The evil wizard is evil for evil's sake.

A different pattern than with the witch is present. Evil wizards are consistently described as almost sadistic villains. They have no idea of morality, like old wise men. Everything is about themselves. If they guard a treasure in the form of a virgin, then it is because they want to possess her, not because they want to enter into a relationship. They do not know feelings like love and do not want to enter into any relationships.

This is clearly seen in the oriental fairy tale *Aladdin and the Wonder-ful Lamp*, a fairy tale of *1001 Arabian Nights* (Silverstein, 1866). In the story, an African magician wants a magic lamp because the spirit in it can fulfil all wishes; however, only a rough diamond can find the lamp. It turns out the street urchin Aladdin is this rough diamond, which is why the wizard captures him to get his power. However, Aladdin defends himself, and can also withstand the powerful magic of the spirit of the lamp. He is more interested in the king's daughter, in contrast to the magician who wants to become the richest and most powerful man and does not care about others.

By 'rough diamond' is probably meant a pure essence, a person who is basically honest and innocent. Although the street urchin Aladdin does not satisfy this condition at first glance, the core of his personality is untarnished.

Implicitly the story is about moderation. Dealing with magical powers is not an easy task and can be done only by a person with moderate char-acteristics – Merlin possesses this ability in the Arthurian legend, but evil wizards normally fall into their megalomania.

The pattern is more or less always the same. The hero or heroine must get to know the magical skills of evil, without identifying with the arche-typal evil. They need to know their own limits, then hide and dupe the evil wizard with trickery and finally destroy him – for example, in the fairy tale *The Old Wizard and His Children* ('Der alte Zauberer und seine Kinder', Keller & Bechstein, 1954) in which two imprisoned children run away, use spells they learned to keep the wizard at a distance, transmute themselves and muck around with him. Finally, they find a safe place in a church where he cannot go (here you can see the connection to the devil). The wizard turns at the end into a cock, and the boy into a fox who grabs and eats the cock.

How can such an evil wizard be seen in a human, e.g. in a grandfather? That might be the case when a grandfather has accumulated a lot of knowledge, but thinks that no one else knows as much as he does – if he takes himself and his experience as the measure of all things and thus falls into megalomania. Such behaviour is unpleasant for others. He sees himself more as a 'saviour', especially when his closest caregivers do not dare to give any more criticism and thus support this process. Jung has described the process of such persons: it could happen that someone slowly but increasingly thinks he is an extraordinary individual; he is very unfriendly or isolated, and finally it becomes increasingly clear to him that he is actually a very important person, a man of great spiritual significance (Jung, 1935, §353). If nobody can stop him, an inflation of his ego happens, and the person is convinced of his great importance to others. If he oppresses his own female part in the form of the anima, the development to the old wise man is hindered, and such a man could become a old, megalomaniac, evil man (Jung, 1934b, §382).

In summary: what impact might such representations have on the child's psyche regarding inner expectations and patterns of meaning, generally internal working models? Developmentally considered, this could mean that these narratives demonstrate to a child that destructive forces are possible and that they could hinder development. The narratives broach generalized relational patterns and provide guidelines for action. As an internal working model, this might mean for a child not to forget in dealing with irrational powerful forces to be smart and clever, so as not to be outwitted, even if the other flies into a rage. Thus, a grandfather could be meant, acting by insisting on his negative and destructive power over the family and putting obstacles in the way of subsequent generations to hinder further development. The narratives could represent an internal working model to the child that one can cope with these forces and that there is a way to handle the uncontrollable narcissistic rage and megalomaniac ideas. From an ontological perspective, the evil wizard affects an entire action, destroys all living things, so that the individual is strongly thrown back on himself. This requires a connection to oneself and to the self and one's own autonomy.

Negative narratives of female images of age

This section will examine what stories, fairy tales, myths and legends there are with negative images of older women to find out what inner expectations and patterns of meaning, generally internal working models may arise. The relationship pattern between older women and young people should be examined to check whether this results in generalized relational patterns.

The archetypal image of the evil witch

In this section we will examine the archetypal image of the 'evil witch', an image that is well represented in European fairy tales such as *Hansel and Gretel* or *The Iron Stove*. Such evil old women may be entirely evil, or only partly angry and partly helpful as in the Russian fairy tale *Baba Yaga*.

Baba Yaga lives in a hut that stands on chicken legs and at an invisible border line that must never be crossed. Baba Yaga and her Hungarian sister, the witch Iron Nose, have two souls in their chest, in which the light and the darkness are not entirely separate. Both are full of forces of chaos, despair and destruction, but also give useful support as they stand close to the power of nature (von Franz, 1977, p. 152).

In the Russian version of Snow White, *Oletschka* (Diederichs, 1955, no. 23), for example, the girl flees from the evil stepmother and comes to a hut on chicken legs and dog feet. Baba Yaga, the old witch, asks the girl: 'Will you come to me willingly or unwillingly?'. 'Not so much with the will, Granny, as against my will and with deep sorrow', is Oletsch-ka's response. She must flee from the stepmother. Baba Yaga gives her something to eat and a bed. But as Baba Yaga also lives with a six-headed dragon, Oletschka leaves quickly the next morning.

In the Russian fairy tale *Vasilisa, the Beautiful* (Afanasyev, 2013), the girl struggles in her meagre life with a wicked stepmother and her two children. Her mother died and at her death she gave the girl a doll as a blessing. When the girl was in need, the doll would advise her. One day her father, a merchant, has to leave the home to travel to a distant place. The stepmother urges Vasilisa to go to Baba Yaga in the forest to fetch fire. With great fear, the girl walks with her doll into the dark forest and comes to a cabin surrounded by a fence made of human bones and skulls. The door handle is a human arm and the door lock a mouth with grinning teeth. The skulls on the post begin to glitter. Seeing this, Vasilisa begins to tremble with fear. Baba Yaga rushes nearby and shouts 'Who is there?'. The girl says 'It is only me, grandmother' (Afanasyev, 2013, p. 14). (This is interesting, Baba Yaga appears also to be a close relative as a grandmother.). Vasilisa says she needs fire. Baba Yaga tells her to stay for a while and serve her, then she will get the fire.

Vasilisa is not scared, but says what she wants. This steadfastness seems to prevent the witch killing her immediately. But she must perform almost impossible tasks, otherwise she will eat her. Vasilisa succeeds only through the magical help of the doll. When Baba Yaga returns and asks if everything is done, the girl responds again, self-confidently, to check herself. Baba Yaga looks everywhere and gets mad because she cannot find anything wrong. She's angry that she has no power over the girl, who can perform overwhelming tasks. But she hides her anger and gives the girl even more impossible tasks the next day, which the girl with the doll manages again. The girl shows no submissiveness, although a permanent threat of death is present.

Finally, the evil witch gives in and allows her to ask her questions, but adds at the same time that she should remember that not all questions are wise. So Baba Yaga has given up killing the girl and allows her to look beyond things, into a world where absolute knowledge lives. This is an archetypal moment of meeting; Baba Yaga allows the girl to participate in something bigger and wiser. The girl is also willing to go beyond her world and to see into a larger world. Baba Yaga warns her not to overdo it. Although the girl has questions, she knows the limits of her power and she does not want to know everything. It seems as if it is only possible for a few moments to look beyond, to gaze into the archetypal world, otherwise there is the risk of inflation.

The doll probably embodies an image of the deeper nature of the mother (von Franz, 1977, p. 146), which is sufficient, together with the blessing of the mother, that Vasilisa can withstand Baba Yaga in view of her possible death. In fear and panic the girl draws on her mother, in addition to a spiritual power, which is expressed by the blessing of the mother. This banishes the destructive power of Baba Yaga so that she becomes a useful natural power that rules over the fire.

When the witch realizes her limits in contact with the child and finds out that the blessing of the mother and the doll are the cause, she changes her mind and gives her fire, which is kept in skulls. When faced with the glowing eyes of the skulls the stepmother and her two daughters die promptly and are burnt to ashes.

An entirely wicked witch is found in the fairy tale *Jorinde and Jorin-gel* (Grimm, 2014, no. 69). There is a witch who lives in an old castle in the middle of a large forest. During the day she transforms herself into a cat or owl; in the evening into a human being. If someone approaches within 100 paces of the castle, he is paralysed until she absolves him. If a virgin comes, she turns her into a bird and locks her in with the other 7,000 birds in the castle.

The beautiful Jorinde comes one day with her fiancé Joringel, unsuspectingly on a walk in the forest; she gets too close to the castle and is bewitched by the owl-witch and turned into a nightingale. Joringel, petrified by the witch, has to watch helplessly, unable to speak or even cry. Night comes and an old hunchbacked woman with red eyes and a hooked nose emerges from behind a bush and says mockingly to Joringel that he will never get her back. Joringel dreams later in the night that he finds a blood-red flower, in the middle of which is a beautiful pearl. What he touches with this flower will be freed from the spell. After a long journey he finds the flower and marches to the witch's castle, and although she breathes fire and brimstone, she cannot prevent him from entering the castle. Secretly she tries to hide the basket with Jorinde, but he looks at her and touches the basket and the old woman with the flower, whereupon Jorinde is free and the witch is paralysed.

The hero or a heroine in a fairy tale sometimes has to interact with such darker aspects of the old in order to develop. The hero and heroine can identify little with this figure; they are very far from their consciousness and daily lives, yet they sometimes only come to the deeper layers of your unconscious if they expose themselves to the evil witch. If they do so unprotected, she sprays her deadly poison.

The wicked witch symbolizes a figure who exudes an inexplicable and invisible effect, a kind of demonic magical influence of the consciousness, with the effect that someone feels paralysed and lifeless. Witches isolate; it is no longer possible to live freely. One gives his dignity and his will (Birkhäuser-Oeri, 1977, p. 89). The witch looks greedy, angry, vengeful, jealous, and shows no aversion to scheming and offensive behaviour. These may be unconscious characteristics of someone they resist to become conscious. If a grandmother is guided by such an archetypal image, future generations can often only defend themselves insufficiently. The grandmother unconsciously destroys the young, lively and vibrant life for reasons of envy and retaining power, and thus bars the young from autonomy.

This is shown in the fairy tale *Rapunzel* (Grimm, 2014, no. 12). The story begins with a woman who is childless, but finally gets pregnant. Behind the house of a widely feared sorceress she sees beautiful rampion (rapunzel); they look so fresh and green that she longs for it very much. Finally, her husband steals it. The man is caught by the witch and has to promise her the unborn child. When the child is born the witch gets her and names her Rapunzel; she locks her up at the top of a tower, and only she is able to go up by calling, 'Rapunzel, Rapunzel, let down your hair'. One day a prince sees this and can finally climb in the same way to reach Rapunzel. The witch is furious because the girl cheated on her, cuts off the girl's hair and is mocking about the king's son. As he wants to visit Rapunzel again, the witch shows him the cut hair and says cruelly that he will never get to the girl. The witch takes Rapunzel into a desert where she has to live in extreme poverty until the prince finds and saves her.

Without going into more detail, I want to pick out the parts that are interesting for our context – namely that this sorceress has a herb whose roots are edible and that reach deep into the earth. Symbolically considered this could be seen as ancestor consciousness, what the young couple would like to have – a reference to the roots – but the couple receives this only if they sacrifice their child. When Rapunzel is aged 12 and at the beginning of puberty, she is imprisoned by the witch in a tower in the forest with neither stairs nor door. The witch tries thus to destroy possible liaisons and the autonomy of the girl; she should remain trapped, be only related to the witch and forget the outside world. The witch represents a self-preserving tendency; youth locked up with no future. The conservative power becomes destructive and blocks Rapunzel's autonomy. The girl cheats on the old woman and has to live in a desert in great grief and misery, and has to start again without the support of helpful ancient forces.

The friendly old woman who becomes a wicked witch

An evil witch may appear at first glance not toxic, but extremely friendly and pampering, such as the witch in the fairy tale *Hansel and Gretel* (Grimm, 2014, no. 15). Hansel and Gretel are left in the forest by their parents because they do not have enough food and so sacrifice the children, leading them deep into the forest and leaving them alone. The two children go on all night and another day from morning till night, but they cannot find their way out of the woods. They are hungry and find nothing but a few berries. They are so tired that they lay down under a tree and fall asleep. They wake up next morning and see a beautiful white bird:

> When it was mid-day, they saw a beautiful snow-white bird sitting on a bough, which sang so delightfully that they stood still and listened to it. And when it had finished its song, it spread its wings and flew away before them, and they followed it until they reached a little

house, on the roof of which it alighted; and when they came quite up to little house they saw that it was built of bread and covered with cakes, but that the windows were of clear sugar. 'We will set to work on that', said Hansel, 'and have a good meal. I will eat a bit of the roof, and thou, Gretel, canst eat some of the window, it will taste sweet'. Gretel leant against the window and nibbled at the panes.

(Grimm, 2014, p. 64)

The two children revel in this food wealth and satisfy their persisting hunger as a soft voice asks 'who is there?'

Suddenly the door opened, and a very, very old woman, who supported herself on crutches, came creeping out. Hansel and Gretel were so terribly frightened that they let fall what they had in their hands. The old woman, however, nodded her head, and said, 'Oh, you dear children, who has brought you here? Do come in, and stay with me. No harm shall happen to you'. She took them both by the hand, and led them into her little house. Then good food was set before them, milk and pancakes, with sugar, apples, and nuts'.

(Grimm, 2014, p. 65)

The children think they are in heaven. But the old woman is known to be a wicked witch, who built the house of gingerbread only to lure children. A giving, nurturing woman turns out to be a deadly witch. With her red eyes she cannot see far, but she has a keen sense of smell, like the beasts. She lures people with paradisiacal images of food to her witch's cottage that even Hansel, who is usually wise, falls for.

The psychoanalyst Carl-Heinz Mallet can imagine that love can pamper so that children get too dependent. He applies the fairy tale *Hansel and Gretel* to mothers who spoil their sons, wash their laundry, iron their shirts and cook the best food while the sisters have to work hard (Mallet, 1987). But even a grandmother can spoil and unconsciously take control over the autonomy of their grandchildren. Such a grandmother understands everything and forgives everything. An exceedingly indulgent grandmother can act like an evil witch, as we shall see in greater detail in the section on Red Riding Hood.

In summary: what impact can such representations have on the child's psyche regarding inner expectations and patterns of meaning, generally internal working models? From the perspective of development psychology this could mean that a child encounters certain persistent, paralysing forces when it meets with its grandmother, who wants to keep the child at a certain level of development and does not want it to grow up. The child who hears the described narratives could deduce as an internal working model that where danger is a person can defend himself. (Wicked witches can then even transform, in contrast to the evil wizards, into supporting figures.) The risk is a grandmother with characteristics such as envy, the inclination to gossip, to slander or making false promises, which poisons the relationship of parents and children. According to such internal working models, a child could use its autonomy to deny these destructive forces, to not be poisoned. Being poisoned may also have ontological dimensions. The wicked witch can affect an entire event and destroy every living thing. A person will be thrown back to himself in order to survive and to get in contact of his self and autonomy (see the clinical section).

Chapter 4

Internal working models, complexes and intersubjectivity

Internal working models and complexes

In the previous chapters the concept of 'internal working models' according to the attachment theory of Bowlby (1969, 1973) was used in order to imagine the effect of narratives on the development of a child. This effect is further investigated in this chapter.

Internal working models include representative information on patterns of relationships and caregiving, and enable a child to endure states without a mother. They contain inner expectations and patterns of meaning. Working models offer to process cognitive information. Attachment theory proposes thus a bridge between psychodynamic theories and cognitive sciences, argues Jean Knox (Knox, 2003).

Internal working models influence far more than just cognitive processes; they also influence perception and the behaviour of a child to significant others. They are often unconscious since they are anchored in implicit memory. Parents communicate their internal working models mostly unconsciously to their children, which has led to the famous statement by the psychoanalyst Selma Fraiberg and her colleagues:

> In every nursery there are ghosts. There are the visitors from unremembered past of the parents, the uninvited guests at the christening. Under all favorable circumstances the unfriendly and unbidden spirits are banished from the nursery and return to their subterranean dwelling place.... This is not to say that ghosts cannot invent mischief from their burial places. Even among families where the love bonds are stable and strong, the intruders from the parental past may break through the magic circle in an unguarded moment, and a parent and his child may find themselves reenacting a moment or a scene from another time with another set of characters.
>
> (Fraiburg *et al.*, 1975, p. 387)

It is an undisputed fact that the internal working models of the parent's act in the nursery. According to Knox you can even go a step further: with the 'Adult Attachment Interview' one can prove in fact that parents have the same internal working models in the form of attachment models as the children in the 'Strange Situations' test (Ainsworth *et al.*, 1978; Knox, 2003). The parents' working models become part of a child's world, which supports the theory of the intergenerational transmission of attachment patterns. However, it seems this relationship is somewhat one-sided. Children learn in later years more and different attachment models (the Strange Situations test is standardized and is carried out on children aged between 12 and 18 months). Also, the reality shows that not all children in a family have the same internal working models; there are differences and variations which depend, *inter alia*, on the position among siblings of a child. The hypothesis is, too, that children can learn different internal models from grandparents.

The notion of internal working models was described first by attachment theorist John Bowlby. The topic has also arisen in analytical psychology with the reflection of the relationship between internal working models and complexes (Bovensiepen, 2006; Knox, 2003). *Complexes* are, simply put, the equivalent in analytical psychology to internal working models. But the question is nevertheless: must we abandon the term *complex*, which belongs to the classical terminology of analytical psychology, and replace it with *internal working models*, or is it still useful for explaining attachment and relationship patterns?

First: what is meant by 'complex'? Nancy Krieger (2014), Erel Shalit (2002) and Verena Kast (1992, 1994) have written excellent books about this topic. For our purposes we will only concentrate on the connection with internal working models.

The term complex comes from the Latin word 'complexus', meaning enclosure, connection or link. C.G. Jung developed the complex theory from 1905 onwards (Jung, 1911). Jolande Jacobi argues that the term complex stems from Jung and was first published in *Diagnostic Association Studies* in 1904/1905. (However, she adds in footnote 2 that Eugen Bleuler also used the term; Jacobi, 1973, p. 54). Freud and Adler also used the term complex, referring to the Oedipus complex (Freud) or the power and inferiority complex (Adler). The complex represents the royal road to the unconscious according to Jung – not dreams as Freud believed (Jung, 1934a).

Jacobi describes the nature of the complex in a small but enlightening chapter: the complex defined by Jung contains emotional parts of the personality, groups of psychic contents that have separated from the consciousness, which work arbitrarily and autonomously (Jacobi, 1973, p. 45). They run a separate existence in the unconscious, from where they can inhibit or promote consciousness at any time. The complex consists primarily of one core element which carries meaning, and is linked with feeling associations (Jacobi, 1973). Jacobi draws a graph that shows the collapse of the consciousness due to the ascending complex. Jung wrote that the individual would be 'taken' from the emotional complex: such a complex 'has its own wholeness and, in addition, a relatively high degree of autonomy' (Jung, 1934a, §201); it is behaving like a foreign body in the consciousness.

However, to be gripped by a complex, a trigger must be present. Only then can a complex be 'constellated':

> This term simply expresses the fact that the outward situation releases a psychic process in which certain contents gather together and prepare for action. When we say that a person is 'constellated' we mean that he has taken up a position from which he can be expected to react in a quite definite way. But the constellation is an automatic process which happens involuntarily and which no one can stop on his own accord.
>
> (Jung, 1934a, §198)

The behaviour is compared to the internal working models more pronounced, because complexes activate not only thoughts but also behaviour such as flight, fight or freeze. In addition, feelings accompany the behaviour – Jung speaks of the 'emotionally charged complex' (Jung, 1934a, §196).

Moreover, if we fall into a complex, cognitions and bodily sensations are activated. In a pronounced complex it seems as if a spirit has gone into the person.

Jung described in 1912, in *Symbols of Transformation*, 'Every split-off portion of libido, every complex, has or is a (fragmentary) personality' (Jung, 1912, §388). This is visible, for example, in the inferiority complex, which brings the individual to an inhibited attitude in which one feels weak and worthless and simultaneously does not understand what is happening. The experience of the ghosts in the nursery may represent a similar experience.

The meaning of the term 'complex' has developed in the common language so that it represents a flaw. However, in the view of analytical psychology by C.G. Jung it first had a neutral meaning: complex can have a healthy or pathogenic aspect (being in love has, for example, all the hallmarks of a complex). In Jungian literature the focus has been placed in recent decades only on the pathological complexes and on the following pathology (Bovensiepen, 2009; Shalit, 2002), which states: complexes are stored in the implicit memory, probably caused by a painful clash of the individual with a request or an event in the environment, where there is no match (Kast, 1992).

Complexes are formed on the basis of personal experiences and fantasies from relationship interactions in childhood and youth that are based on archetypal experiences that revolve around the same cultural issues and experiences. The perception in terms of similar events in adulthood is thereby disturbed. The adult shows whether complexes 'start' exaggerated thoughts, emotions and bodily reactions (Haule, 2011). The behaviour is often not adjusted, but stereotyped and runs automatically. The reaction proceeds just like a reflex.

Another – intersubjective – feature that should be mentioned is the power of the constellation. Not only the one who has 'fallen' into a complex, he also pulls the other into the constellation process. His perception, emotions, bodily sensations and behaviour are influenced whether he wants it or not. The complex forces the other more or less into the complex events, depending on the strength. The Berliner Hans Dieckmann even spoke of a 'force field' that a complex can constellate (Dieckmann, 1991).

An example: someone with an authority complex can create an atmosphere that makes it difficult for open communication with his supervisor. Even he can be inhibited because he no longer knows what he may say not to worry his subordinate.

In this example two other features of the complex are mentioned: the identification and the projection of the complex (see also Dieckmann, 1991; Jacobi, 1959). Kast extended this classification and separated the victim identification from the perpetrator identification (Kast, 1994). Either you behave like the wounded child or as the punitive parent.

Already these few lines show that the concept of the complexes is broader than the concept of internal working models. In particular, we need to keep in mind its intersubjective effect when it is said that we 'fall' into a complex, a complex 'is constellated' or a complex 'is projected'. This language refers to what is happening with complexes in a particular situation with a triggering stimulus. The intrapsychic patterns are thus carried in a certain way in a relationship with the other. (Complexes emerge also in the therapy and in the analysis in the form of transference and countertransference. The complex organization of both needs to be kept in mind.)

Another, more intrapsychic, element of the complex concerns the dissociation aspect. Jung's conception of the psyche is based on the dissociability of the psyche. Pierre Janet had made him familiar with this view as Jung deepened his training as a psychiatrist in his hospital, Hôpital de la Salpêtrière in Paris. Jung suggested that experiences are not always stored in the same way in the memory. In a psyche different 'splinter psyches' are at work as complexes, as Jung described in his article 'A review of the Complex Theory': 'Today we can take it as moderately certain that complexes are in fact "splinter psyches"' (Jung, 1934a, §204). 'These fragments subsist relatively independently of one another and can take one another's place at any time, which means that each fragment possesses a high degree of autonomy' (Jung, 1934a, §202).

The Jungian Gustav Bovensiepen deepened our understanding of this dissociability of the psyche and brought infant research, the neurosciences and the object relations theory closer to the concept of complexes and internal working models (Bovensiepen, 2006). Bovensiepen understands the complexes as Jung does the splinter psyches, as a dissociated sub-network within the network structure of the psyche, which work together with internal working models, characteristic affects and unconscious expectation fantasies. This network model even allows us to understand defence organizations as a pathological organization of complexes. Jung proposed, according to Bovensiepen, a vertical split in different psyches that contains conscious and unconscious parts. As Knox, Bovensiepen thinks the dissociated schema can be viewed as an internal working model. The complex contains an archetypal core (e.g. archetypal attachment expectation), mental representations and sensomotory and affective experiences. There are various complexes (and various internal working models) that are stored in the implicit memory. (A positive grandfather complex may stand unconnected next to a negative father complex.)

Therefore, Bovensiepen defines the complex as follows:

> I imagine then *a complex* to be a limited section, a *sub-network* from the entire fabric of intersubjective experiences. The reach of this sub-network could be limited by three factors:

1 through a string of similar, but not exact, internal working models,
2 through a similar *affective colouring* or a set of emotions and
3 through certain *expectation patterns* relating to outer objects.

(Bovensiepen, 2006, p. 458)

Such a complex works as a basic unit of the psyche.

Bovensiepen brought in with this definition a broader view of the complexes than Knox, who views complexes just as analogous to internal working models while Bovensiepen sees complexes rather as a subnetwork of all internalized experiences of a child which are stored in the implicit memory and consist of internal working models, emotions and patterns of expectation. They are partly conscious, but mostly unconscious (Bovensiepen, 2006).

The complex model of Bovensiepen makes sense. Each unit has its own emotions, cognitive representations, perceptions, expectation fantasies, defences, behaviour and memories that can be projected or with which one can identify (see also Meier, 2013). These are unconscious mental structures, unconnected to each other, which distort the current reality in order to correspond with the previously experience.

In my view the concept of the internal working models is in a certain respect more helpful than the term complexes: whereas the last one summarizes similar emotions, cognitions, perception and bodily sensations, the notion of the internal working model is more undifferentiated, but comprehensive. Someone may be able to have one complex but many more working models. A child, for example, may develop a working model with his grandfather, but not necessarily a complex. To a complex belong exaggerated, distorted emotions and patterns of expectation, but these do not necessarily belong to the internal working model. A child may say 'With this grandfather I have a good experience when I listen to him because he is telling me a lot of stories'. Working models seem to have more to do with information processing and cognitive patterns, complexes more with feelings and with distorted, simplified perceptions, cognitions, emotions and behaviours that generate a forcefield and therefore stress a more dynamic aspect compared to internal working models. The complex concept of analytical psychology approaches the notion of schema therapy (see also Meier, 2013).

Complex, intersubjectivity theory and the present moment

We now leave the Jungian debate and turn to the psychoanalytic discussion. The reason is that the above-mentioned debate revealed the intersubjective level of the complex. In order to activate a complex a trigger is usually needed. A complex is 'constellated' due to a property of a person, a smell, an impression, an event, an unconscious perception, etc. These have the effect that the person 'falls into' his complex and reacts stereotypically. Automatic complex reactions take place and a forcefield is constellated. However, these intersubjective processes are not addressed in the Jungian debate.

The intersubjectivity debate has emerged in recent years from the research of psychoanalysts. The so-called relational psychoanalysts link together intrapsychic and intersubjective processes – which means subjective processes in the person and processes between persons. This is in contrast to Freud and the orthodox psychoanalysts, who are only interested in processes in the person.

That means what? Results of infant research, systems theorists and the neurosciences have been included in the psychoanalytic approach, in the sense that intersubjective processes between two persons (child–caregiver, two adults, patient–therapist, etc.) are examined in more detail. It was found that even babies join their mothers in a 'head dance', in a synchronized rhythm of speech, voice modulation, the strength of the voice, changes in body posture, breathing, facial expression, eye contact and gestures (e.g. Beebe & Lachmann, 2002). Trevarthen has described these early forms of intersubjectivity in a series of publications (Trevarthen, 1999/2000). The infant and the mother react within a split-second; even if they are in two different rooms and see each other only through screens, both react to movement and facial expressions and anticipate the intentions of the other. An overview of these investigations in given by Stern (2004).

Thus an implicit relational knowledge of intersubjective processes with relevant others is developed in the child. The renowned developmental psychologist and psychoanalyst Daniel Stern and the Boston Change Process Study Group (a study group consisting of psychoanalysts, childhood researchers, paediatricians, psychiatrists and analytical theorists) published several articles about this. He indicates these events as a co-constructive process between child and caregiver (Stern, 2000, 2004). A rule-based set of expectations is the basis of the implicit relational knowledge of the child and is procedurally encoded before the symbolic language emerges. It includes the normal as well as pathological knowledge, and integrates emotions, fantasies, (body) behavioural and cognitive dimensions (Lyons-Ruth, 1998). This type of knowledge is becoming more differentiated, articulated and integrated (Gotthold & Sorter, 2006) over the years.

What does this mean in relation to our topic? A child with a strict mother receives relational knowledge in dealing with her, which is expressed in body language, the tone of voice, eye contact, emotions, etc. In Jungian terms: the child develops a mother complex. With a loving grandfather, however, another relational knowledge exists, with a different body language and different emotional expression. In Jungian terms: the child develops a positive grandfather complex. With a negative mother complex, emotions, cognitions, behaviour and expectations are consistent with each other, and rather negative. The same child but has another set of positive emotions, cognitions, behaviour expressions and expectations in a positive grandparent complex.

This is not only the view of analytical psychology. The view, namely that the psyche has not a uniform inner structure, is also represented by the psychotherapy researcher Eugene Georgaca. She argues that the psyche is designed in dialogue, as a constellation of dialogical structured positions, each of which has its own vision of the world and its own voice in contexts of intersubjective exchange and dominance. The ego moves between positions in an imago landscape depending on time, place and situation; a chorus of self is the result (Georgaca, 2001, p. 224). The theory of intersubjectivity includes far more still.

The research group led by Daniel Stern emphasized that intersubjectivity not only takes place at intervals, but without pause, second by second. He sees intersubjectivity as a fundamental state of relations and thus represents a broader perspective of intersubjectivity than others (e.g. Beebe & Lachmann, 2002; Orange, Atwood & Stolorow, 2001). Stern even suspects that intersubjectivity is a human universal and innate basic need, a basal motivation system, and completes the motivation system of attachment (Stern, 2004). Autistic children, for example, are able to engage in attachment behaviour, but not intersubjective behaviour.

He and his research group gather criteria in a phenomenological approach that occurs in the intersubjective space as the present moment, the now moment and the moment of meeting.

These terms play an important role for this study because they bring in, on the one hand, the archetypal moment in the debate, and provide, on the other hand, a model of what is happening with the relational know-ledge, with the complexes or internal working models in the intersubjec-tive field.

Characteristics of the present moment

- The present moment (Stern, 2004) is a subjective experience of what is happening in a specific, short period of time. It is experienced; the moment is not told.
- The experience is either new or problematic and therefore enters into consciousness. The moment breaks through the ordinary and requires mental activity to solve the 'problem'. Both partners move to a hidden target while the present moment is gone through. It needs mental work, because one has constantly to deal with what is hap-pening in a nascent change moment. One tries to 'read' the thoughts, feelings and body posture of the other.
- The present moment has a holistic shape, and organizes sequences or groups of small, imperceptible units. It consists of a succession of actions, postures, perceptions and sensations.
- While the present moment unfolds it is not exactly predictable how it ends. The two parties use co-creativity to mend any breaks, but whether this will be successful cannot be predicted.

Now moment as a specific present moment

There are present moments, in which the status quo of the relationship is at risk and both sides accept the intersubjective field is shaken. Stern says this moment has a *Kairos* quality. (With *Kairos* the Greeks designated the opportune moment, the moment when something new turns up, looming, or a moment arises that represents a confluence of events, after which an action is possible.) Stern calls this moment as the now moment:

- Certain elements of the past are activated in the now moment, but there is a new context, something is regrouped or replaced. The now moment contains very dynamic processes.
- Gotthold and Sorter (2006) have described the now moment in psychotherapy: they state that surprise accompanies a now moment, as a space opens and the state of the other is shared between the two. Implicitly both understand the other without necessary interpretation. However, a self-regulation is necessary, since a certain restlessness

of one's own state is expected. Depending on how the now moment goes, it could have consequences for the future. Even Stern thinks that a now moment threatens the existing intersubjective field in therapy. A renegotiation is on the table and could cause a strong emotional charge in the atmosphere. The therapist feels disarmed, unprepared; he does not know what to do, but feels very present.

- There are rare and outstanding now moments, after which life strikes in a different direction. This can be seen as a 'moment of truth', as a 'great moment' or as a 'decisive moment' (Stern, 2004). Barthes' '*punctum*' is probably also a now moment. From a Jungian perspective we would speak of an 'archetypal present moment' in which an archetype pushes into the foreground.

Jean Knox suggests a scale as a metaphor to illustrate the emergence of a now moment. On one side in a weighing pan is a gradually increasing weight of new internal working models, which are formed in therapy; on the other side is a pan with the gradually decreasing weight of the old working models, which lose their force. A now moment could be the point at which the scales with the new internal working models suddenly lower and the other pan loses steam. Jean Knox proposed the metaphor to Daniel Stern at a conference in 2002 and he confirmed it as a possible explanation of the relation between the now moment and gradual changes in internal working models (Knox, 2003, p. 189).

Moment of meeting as a specific present moment

A now moment makes a moment of meeting necessary, since this solves the challenge posed by the now moment crisis. If a moment of meeting can take place, this can be remembered even years later.

- In the crisis of the now moment both psyches create islands of intentionality which move the intersubjective field. Stern takes into these considerations the theory of dynamical systems (Thelen & Smith, 1998). The two psyches create new emergent properties. Due to the desire for an intersubjective contact, both mobilize a co-creativity and let the new emergent properties arise that alter the parties.
- The solution is carried out by moments of meeting as a well-coordinated response to the crisis of the now moment. It is a moment that implicitly reorganized the intersubjective field, so that its consistency is growing and both parties perceive an opening of their

relationship that allows them to jointly explore implicit or explicit new areas (Stern, 2004).

• After a successful moment of meeting, the intersubjective field has increased, the implicit relationship is rearranged and follows the new possibilities. What has been experienced can enter into long-term memory and is part of an association network. An association thread is embedded in the present moment, from which an association network can form.

German-speaking psychoanalysts have addressed these considerations (Jaenicke, 2006). Lilian Otscheret and Claus Braun published considerations about intersubjective processes in analytical psychology (Otscheret & Braun, 2005). From a Jungian perspective it can be assumed that a present moment arises when the analyst does not accept a complex transference, which can give the analysis in a co-constructive process a new turn.

The English Jungian Jean Knox has intervened in the debate and brought in the term 'turn-taking' (Knox, 2012). With this term she means mutual give and take, which in any communication plays a crucial role as a kind of Ariadne's thread, ensuring human exchange. Turn-taking can be observed in mother–child interactions as well as in an analytic session. An act of a person produces a reaction in the other, after which the latter reacts so that the characteristics of human action and interaction can be constructed, which gives the basis for the co-construction of the self. Turn-taking processes are essential for the development of the feeling that one exists.

Knox refers to a definition of Horst Hendriks-Jansen who regards turn-taking as an emergent phenomenon, which itself serves as a scaffold or dynamic context for advanced patterns. It can be thought of as a nucleus in which meaning unfolds (Hendriks-Jansen, 1996, p. 277). Knox combines Hendriks-Jansen's action and meaning as essential features of the turn-taking process, in which both try to interact and to repair if the interaction fails. But why is the action ultimately so important?

The moment of interaction is now given more space and weight in theoretical discussions. Stern and his study group go so far as to think that present moments can influence the past. The past is something happening in the present:

> The notion of *the present remembering context* is widely accepted in thinking about memory.... In brief, memory is not viewed as a

library of experiences where the first editions are kept in their original form and one of them can be called up and pulled into the present as a memory to be relived faithfully. Instead, memory is viewed as a collection of fragments of experiences. These get turned into a whole remembered experience in the following way. Events and experiences going on at the present time act as a context (a present remembering context) that selects, assembles, and organizes the fragments into a memory. The present remembering context is whatever is happening now on the mental stage in this present moment. This can include a smell, a sound, a melody, a word, a face, the quality of light, internal feeling states, bodily feelings, a thought, and so on.

(Stern, 2004, p. 198)

Fragments of the past can therefore be reassembled in the present. Stern asks, supported by neuroanatomical studies in rabbits, whether it is not possible that every present moment rewires the neural recording of the past and reformulates the memories of the past (Stern, 2004 p. 201). Thus, originals do not exist any longer and the past is permanently rewritten. However, a moment of meeting could only change the past in small doses, says Stern. It can also be said that Stern's database is somewhat meagre; this would need further research.

In summary, Bruschweiler-Stern *et al.* (2007) argue that it is not so much the intrapsychic events that determine what happens on the interactional level, but the interactive process itself that is primary and provides the raw material, derived from the generalized abstractions such as conflict, defence or unconscious fantasies (I would add the complexes to this list). Conflicts and defence are born in interaction and these constitute the deeper level of experience, while the abstractions that we use for the repetitive aspects of the relationship strategies are secondary descriptions of the lower levels, but not the level itself (Bruschweiler-Stern *et al.* 2007, p. 14). This places the intersubjective/interactional over the intrapsychic level. In Jungian terms: complexes can only be activated when a trigger exists.

The developmental psychologists Ester Thelen and Linda Smith of the University of Indiana argue similarly:

We propose here a radical departure from the current cognitive theory. Although behavior and development appear structured, there are no rules. Although behavior and development appear rule-driven, there are no rules. There is complexity. There is a multiple, parallel and continuously dynamic interplay of perception and action and a system that, by its thermodynamic nature, seeks certain stable solutions. These solutions emerge from relations, not from design. Then the elements of such complex systems cooperate, they give rise to behavior with a unitary character, and thus to the illusion of structure. But the order is always executory, rather than rule-driven, allowing for the enormous sensitivity and flexibility of behavior to organize and regroup around task and context.

(Thelen & Smith, 1998, p. xix)

The intersubjective level is thus greatly enhanced, now depending on environmental factors. This view was brought into the Jungian understanding of therapeutic processes and some similarities are observable, as we see in the emergence debate among Jungians, the intersubjectivity debate among psychoanalysts and the research of developmental psychologists. The environment and system factors in the form of intersubjective processes has become more valuable for our therapeutic understanding than purely intrapsychic processes (Cambray & Carter, 2004). Present moments and moments of meeting arise in an intersubjective process because of human biology, the environment and the narrative. This means in Jungian terms an archetypal image or archetypal present moment can emerge. This will be described in the following chapter.

Chapter 5

Archetypal present moments

The story of 'Heidi': Heidi and her grandfather

In the world literature there is a fine example in which you can identify archetypal moments between a grandfather and a grandchild, as well as the dependence of the encounter of intersubjective processes, archetypal constellations and patterns of expectation.

It is a story that a few years after the first publication became an international success and has been translated into 50 languages and made into a film. In countries such as Switzerland, Japan or Turkey this story is one of the most important works of children's literature. We are talking about the Heidi books or the two books *Heidi's Years of Learning and Travel* and *Heidi Makes Use of What She Has Learned* by Swiss author Johanna Spyri (1827–1901) from the years 1880 and 1881. About 50 million copies have been sold since the first publication of the book. Spyri wrote the story at a time that big social changes and political upheaval was taking place in Switzerland. Rural areas were overrun by industrialization and many classes were impoverished. This led to a rural exodus, an emigration wave, alcoholism and unemployment. This atmosphere built created the background. I think the story from the nineteenth century is well known and will mention only a few basics here (Spyri, 2007 [1899]).

Heidi is a 5-year-old orphan girl who is brought to her reclusive grandfather in the village of Maienfeld in the canton of Graubünden, in the Alps. Heidi's parents both died early, and she was raised by her aunt in town. For several reasons the child is too troublesome for her. She hardly takes care of the girl because she has to work in a factory; in the evenings she is tired and so the child is left to her own devices. Eventually, she decides that she cannot carry on like this. She remembers her grandfather, and since he is related to the girl he should also be responsible for her. The 70-year-old *Alpöhi* (Swiss for grandfather) lives alone in his mountain chalet. The problem, however, is that he is known in the village as a difficult and unfriendly person.

When the villagers hear that the little girl will come to this fellow they are horrified. They argue that he has a very bad reputation; no one wants to have anything to do with him. Everyone avoids him when he comes to the village once each year to exchange his cheese for other food.

The Alpöhi was formerly an aggressive, impulsive bully. He was supposed to take over the family farm as he was the firstborn, but he did not take this responsibility seriously; he gambled away the farm and engaged in brawls and binge drinking and got into bad company. When the farm had to be sold, his father and his mother died of grief. The Alpöhi sought his fortune in Italy since he had lost his reputation and money. It was said that he had served as a soldier in Naples and killed people. After a few years he came back with a teenage boy – Heidi's father – but no one wanted to have anything more to do with him. That annoyed him very much and he retired, stubborn and grim, to the Alps, where he lived secluded and did goat herding. His son learned a skill, married a woman who gave birth to Heidi, but he was then killed by a falling beam. Soon after, the woman died from grief.

The small, emotionally neglected girl has to go to this Alpöhi now. It is understandable that the villagers react in horror, but the aunt says the Alpöhi must take care of the child – it is his responsibility. The villagers argue further that one should be afraid of him. He looks scary with his thick grey eyebrows and his beard. He doesn't talk with anyone and he lives in discord with God and the people. They are afraid for the little girl. Everyone thinks the grim grandfather could mistreat her, neglect her even more than she already has been.

Let us recall the innate, unsaturated archetypal patterns of expectation, namely that the environment should meet the expectations of attachment (Bisagni, 2009). Unsaturated means that there is no experience of love, loyalty or empathy. The girl's archetypal expectations of loyalty, her need to be heard, seen and understood, were not yet saturated. She was indeed rather pushed around. Her grandfather showed narcissistic-impulsive behaviour in previous years, which suggests that his emotional attachment needs were insufficiently satisfied by his parents. But the archetypal expectation patterns are always there, even if they are unsaturated.

The following occurs in the story:

Heidi was at the top first. She went straight up to the old man, put out her hand and said: 'Good evening, Grandfather' – 'So, so what is the meaning of this?' he asked gruffly, as he gave the child an abrupt shake of the hand, and gazed long and scrutinising at her from under his bushy eyebrows. Heidi stared steadily back at him in return with unflinching gaze for the grandfather, with his long beard and the thick grey eyebrows that grew together over his nose and looked just like a brush, was such a remarkable appearance, that Heidi was unable to take her eyes off him.

(Spyri, 2007, p. 10)

What happens? Heidi does not know the grandfather's past, not even the rumours, conversations and projections of the village people. Her grandfather again tries to respond, as he is used to being alone and wants to keep the child at a distance in order to create distance from negative assessments, but it is not working. The child finds his eyebrows interesting, not scary, and she carefully looks at them.

What happens next?

As soon as Dete [the aunt] had disappeared, the old man went back to his bench, and there he remained seated, staring on the ground without uttering a sound, while thick curls of smoke floated upward from his pipe. Heidi, meanwhile, was enjoying herself in her new surroundings; she looked about till she found a shed, built against the hut, where the goats were kept; she peeped in, and saw it was empty. She continued her search ... and went on again, to the farther corner of the hut, and so round to where her grandfather was sitting. Seeing that he was in exactly the same position as when she left him, she went and placed herself in front of the old man, and putting her hands behind her back, stood and gazed at him.

(Spyri, 2007, p. 13)

Daniel Stern said that the desire for intersubjective contact mobilizes the co-creativity of the two psyches. The scene can be interpreted as a present moment when something happens, what breaks through the ordinary and requires mental activity. The grandfather tried 'to read' the thoughts and feelings of the girl who in turn 'reads' something in the grandfather's face; however, she sees something different than the villagers. The intersubjective field is unsettling, at least for the grandfather. The girl wants to see something interesting; after all, she probably had too little diversion with her aunt. A now moment emerges, 'when the current state of the implicit relational knowing is sharply thrown into question and basic assumptions about the relationship are placed at stake' (Stern, 2004, p. 165). A new state emerges, and this has consequences for the future.

Grandfather asks Heidi, shocked and harshly, what her greeting meant and looks at the child piercingly. Heidi returns the long gaze, persevering and unblinking, because she is curious. Grandfather must then sit on the bench; this is very unexpected and he does not say a word. As Heidi returns from walking around the house, she sees him in the same position as she left him, she stands before him, puts her hands behind her back and looks at him.

An important change is under way in the intersubjective field; the atmosphere is emotionally charged. One suspects confusion and wonder for the grandfather and curiosity and interest for the child. The grandfather does not know how to react; he is quite irritated. The child's behaviour is not similar to what he knows. That upsets him and puts him in the area of another behaviour. Stern says about those moments that one floats equally in the past, present and future (Stern, 2004, p. 28).

The grandfather looks up. 'What is it you want?' he asks, as the child stands motionless before him. 'Come then!' And the grandfather stands up and goes into the hut. Presumably, both have experienced an archetypal present moment that ends in a moment of meeting. 'Bring your bundle of clothes in with you', says the old man to the child. 'I shan't want them anymore', says Heidi. The old man turns around and looks intently at the child, whose black eyes gleam in anticipation of the things that could be in there (Spyri, 2007, p. 13).

Again the girl does not see the piercing eyes, but is very excited in anticipation of all the new things. Where will she sleep, what is there to eat, what is this and that called? Heidi runs after the grandfather, assailing him with a thousand questions and overrunning his defences quite easily. Bit by bit he abandons his grumpiness and resistance. As Heidi was unable to carry a heavy blanket, he willingly took it and placed it on the bed for the child. Heidi is happy about everything after a long period of deprivation. The archetypal pattern of expectation of a positive attachment begins to be saturated for the grandfather as well as for the child.

> In the middle of the night the grandfather got up. 'The child will be frightened'. He murmured half aloud. He mounted the ladder and went and stood by the child's bed. Outside the moon was struggling with the dark, fast-driving clouds, which at one moment left it clear and shining, and the next swept over it, and all again was dark. Just

now the moonlight was falling through the round window straight on to Heidi's bed. She lay under the heavy coverlid, her cheeks rosy with sleep, her head peacefully resting on her little round arm, and with a happy expression on her baby face as if dreaming of something pleasant. The old man stood looking down on the sleeping child until the moon again disappeared behind the clouds and he could see no more, then he went back to bed.

(Spyri, 2007, p. 18)

The conjured crisis probably created a moment of meeting. This happened implicitly and does not have to be verbalized. The mutuality of this moment creates a new intersubjective field, which makes it possible in the relationship to pursue a new field, as yet unknown, but a good direction. When such crises are solved, experiences can be categorized in a different direction than has been the case so far – as a new unconscious processes and behaviour pattern (Bovensiepen, 2006).

In this story, through the archetypal moment of meeting, the grandfather becomes a positive attachment figure for Heidi as Heidi projects onto him the archetypal image of the old man. He always gives an answer to her thousand questions. Grandfather can do everything, Heidi is convinced. He makes benches, spoons and plates, always surrounded by the girl. He will for certain help Goat-Peter's (the boy who raises goats) blind grandmother to make sure her cottage does not fall apart, something that would previously never have occurred to him. Heidi forces the grandfather through his boundless trust into a new behaviour; he exceeds his conscious attitude and assumes the expectation of the child that he is an old wise man. He loses his unsociability, starts to help and to be interested in the fate of his fellow men. He even begins to go to church. Heidi had for the first time in her life a person who responded to her attachment needs and curiosity.

Later, the child is taken away from him, whereupon he promptly falls back into the old pattern of an aggressive, solitary man – until the child returns. The archetype of attachment is saturated in this special grandparent–grandchild relationship. It can be assumed that the archetypal image of the old wise man is activated in different moments of meeting for Heidi. After successful moments of meeting, the intersubjective field has grown and new emergent properties have arisen between him and Heidi. What has been experienced can go into long-term memory and can help both Heidi and the grandfather to a secure attachment that both had been missing.

The fairy tale *Little Red Riding Hood*: Little Red Riding Hood and her grandmother

In the following, another fine example of an archetypal present moment between a grandmother and her grandchild is described. However, the story does not contain a positive archetypal image of a grandmother, but a negative. This is in the fairy tale *Little Red Riding Hood*. Of course, many interpretations of the tale are possible – the following is just one of the possible interpretations.

The Brothers Grimm published the story in the first volume of their fairy tales from 1812 (Donde, 1989). The fairy tale was first published in 1697 by Charles Perrault under the title 'Le Petit Chaperon Rouge' (Perrault, 1697). *Little Red Riding Hood* is one of the most frequently reviewed and interpreted tales.

I assume the story is known and will only focus on a few points. The tale begins:

> Once upon a time there was a little village girl, the prettiest that had ever been seen. Her mother doted on her. Her grandmother was even fonder.
>
> (Donde, 1989, p. 4)

There was nothing that the grandmother would not have given to the child! She spoilt her, as many grandmothers might do. The tale continues: '... and made her a little red hood, which became her so well, that everywhere she went by the name of Little Red Riding Hood' (Donde, 1989, p. 4). In contrast to Heidi, the innate archetypal patterns of expectation of attachment (Bisagni, 2009) were fulfilled with Red Riding Hood. She does not want to do anything else but wear the red cap, which means that the child gladly accepts the pampering. Grandmother and Little Red Riding Hood are on the same wavelength. As a limitation it must be added that the child loses her name and is given a name, which is characterized by the grandmother.

In the fairy tale, the mother requests that the child should bring some cake to the grandmother, who lives in the forest. Little Red Riding Hood makes her way through the forest, but now begins to think independently and to act autonomously. She wants to bring a fresh bouquet to her grandmother and therefore wanders from the path and is late. One possible interpretation is that Little Red Riding Hood grows out of the child's status of obedience and becomes a youth. Although she wants to do something nice for her grandmother, it's an independent decision to deviate from the path. When she has gathered her bouquet she continues on. Little Red Riding Hood is surprised when she finds the grandmother's door open.

When she comes into the room she has such a strange feeling:

> 'Grandmother, dear', she exclaimed. 'What big arms you have!' – 'The better to embrace you, my child'. – 'Grandmother, dear, what big legs you have!' – 'The better to run with, my child!' – 'Grandmother, dear, what big ears you have!' – 'The better to hear with, my child!'
>
> (Donde, 1989, p. 5)

The intersubjective field is unsettling for Little Red Riding Hood. The existing situation breaks through the familiar and has become unclear. Little Red Riding Hood does not recognize the grandmother and starts to ask. She attempts 'to read' her grandmother's appearance. Little Red Riding Hood has to deal with what appears to have changed. A present moment exists in which the implicit knowledge that Little Red Riding Hood has of her grandmother has become questionable. The basic assumptions about the relationship are unsettling:

> 'Grandmother, dear, what big teeth you have!' – 'The better to eat you with!'
>
> (Donde, 1989, p. 5)

The intensity of emotions has increased tremendously. The youthful Little Red Riding Hood sees a completely different grandmother and this confirms her new awareness, namely, that she no longer corresponds to the previous positive archetypal image of a grandmother and has become a negative. Little Red Riding Hood has a wolfish-looking wicked witch in front of her, who wants to devour her. The grandmother confirms her clingy (but destructive) bond by confessing to the girl that she can hear, see and grab better. Because:

> With these words the wicked Wolf leapt upon Little Red Riding Hood and gobbled her up.
>
> (Donde, 1989, p. 5)

The intersubjective field is destroyed, a moment of meeting is not possible to get out of the crisis of the moment, so that the relationship could have continued in a positive way. While in the story of Heidi a moment of meeting grows from a present moment, this does not happen here. The present moment ends in a crisis; Little Red Riding Hood is swallowed, i.e. intersubjectivity is massively destroyed – in an archetypal present moment. Only later Little Red Riding Hood is rescued, and the wolf as a symbol for a too-clingy grandmother, by means of a trick, is over-powered. The hunter places stones – symbol for the infertility of this type of relationship – in the belly so that the wolf finally dies.

Her autonomy efforts help Little Red Riding Hood to come out from a pampering relationship with her grandmother by being aware and addressing her altered appearance. The grandmother confirms her devouring and ultimately destructive relationship offer. Perhaps the girl's new awareness helps the grandmother to drop this side of her and just let it die, since the child is growing up and wants to defend her autonomy. The grandmother has probably noticed that she has too big ears, eyes, a too big mouth for the child so that she becomes too devouring, otherwise she would not have admitted it.

The tale could be further interpreted, as many facets show here. The point, however, is to show what an archetypal present moment between two protagonists looks like, how it is 'resolved' and how the two are later in a completely new state.

Chapter 6

Social significance of the grandparent–grandchild relationship

'Until the end of the world'

You want to know absolutely everything
You want to understand absolutely everything
Some day you will know, some day you will understand
Because you will know and understand
You will know and understand it little by little
You want to hop, you want to run
want to know every bird
want to stand naked in the stream
digging with the excavator
running around, hurrying home
first float some nuts and branches down the stream
over the bridge and even the stairs
you always want me to carry you
you are heavy, I am an old man
it doesn't matter to you, when I suffer
you want to now give commands
You shout: carry me! And I say: yes!
      (Tinu Heiniger, song 'Bis a ds Ändi vo der Wält')

Sociological studies

In an excursus, reference is made to the social meaning of the grandparent–grandchild relationship as seen in the current research. The theme of this book includes a multigenerational perspective with the transgenerational relationships many social scientists are occupied with (sociologists, educators, psychologists, family counsellors and therapists). The literature about the grandparent–grandchild relationship has rapidly grown in recent years (not only in research; this special relationship is sung about even in songs – see the song above from the famous Swiss songwriter Tinu Heiniger). This calls for an explanation: The reasons are, on the one hand, sociodemographic and economic ones: grandparents died in the mid-twentieth century much earlier than today. With longer life expectancy, a longer period in which grandparents are active and healthy and the frequent employment of the mother, grandparents can spend more time with their grandchildren. An ageing society also means that the percentage of grandparents and great-grandparents in a population is increasing.

According to a recent study conducted by the German Youth Institute, every third child up to 3 years old spends at least several hours once each week with the grandmother or grandfather. Two-thirds of parents sporadically ask their own fathers and mothers to babysit (Hüsken *et al.*, 2008). American studies also indicate that from 1982 to 1992 the percentage of children who were co-supervised by grandparents rose, for black children by 24 per cent and for white children by 54 per cent (Caputo, 2001, p. 541). In another study, it was estimated that today about 94 per cent of older adults in the United States take on the social role of grandparents (Hooyman & Kiyak, 1988). Other studies also point to the increase in grandparent participation in child-rearing (Chase Goodman & Silverstein, 2001).

There are mainly psychosocial reasons as to why grandparent care is used. Grandparents offer, especially, in times of crisis such as unemployment, accidents, separation, divorce or chronic illness, important support through practical help and emotional attention (Hank & Buber, 2007; Lussier, Deater-Deckard, Dunn & Davies, 2002). In a recent study of young Americans by Ruiz and Silverstein (2007), it was found that a close and supportive relationship with grandparents helped to reduce depressive symptoms in young people in whose families a parent was lacking. An American study also pointed out that grandmother offered some protection especially to grandchildren who had to endure a lot of frustrations due to their parents. The risk of children developing low social competence was reduced if grandmothers were involved (Neppl, Ontai & Conger, 2010).

Since divorce and remarriage rates have risen and social upheaval progressed rapidly, grandparents represent in many families a stable factor when, for example, stepsisters and stepbrothers enter the picture (Lussier *et al.*, 2002). I remember the example of a young client who was very successful and was sent by her company abroad to many countries. Her parents separated when she was 6 years old and they later divorced. Both parents remarried, and in both families there were additions to the family, which resulted in a frequent change of residence until the new situation stabilized. Throughout these changes only her grandparents remained stable; year after year they lived in the same place and nothing changed. They were her main anchor, more so than her parents.

Other studies show that greater involvement of grandparents is correlated with fewer emotional problems and stronger pro-social behaviour in grandchildren. Youth from single-parent or stepfamilies have fewer adjustment problems if grandparents take care of them than those from intact families (Attar-Schwartz et al., 2009).

Furthermore, the importance of family feeling should be emphasized. Family therapists defines it as a feeling that is necessary in order to ensure the balance between the individual wishes and the needs of the family system to be maintained and cohesive (Reich, Massing & Cierpka, 2007, p. 15). A family feeling ensures that an individual can unconsciously develop an internal image of the family as a whole, in which the individual grows up. Through this inner image a new family can later be started. The family feeling leads to a family identity and a handing down of social and family norms, ideologies and values. However, these need to be sufficiently flexible in order to avoid solidification of the family taking place.

The significance of the grandparents' role in research

The famous Swiss sociologist and gerontologist François Höpflinger argues that grandparents' role is among the few positive connotations of old age. In the biggest qualitative Swiss investigation as part of the National Research Programme 'Kindheit, Jugend und Generationenbeziehungen im gesellschaftlichen Wandel' (Childhood, Youth and Intergenerational Relationships in Social Change) he questioned around 700 students and 600 grandparents about their relationship with each other. The result: from both sides, for nine out of ten respondents the relationship is important to them (Höpflinger, Hummel & Hugentobler, 2006). What does that mean? The majority of grandchildren characterized their grandparents as loving, generous and companionable, a minority as strict and impatient. Most important to them was that grandparents are simply there, listening and available. The most common shared activity mentioned by teenage grandchildren was discussions; second place was watching television together. But teenagers also mentioned issues that are avoided in conversations with grandparents: being in love, the intimate aspects and 'secrets' such as smoking, alcohol consumption and stealing (Höpflinger *et al.*, 2006).

In general, the authors conclude that grandparents are from early on familiar with the child, and yet are noticeably different to the parents. They can assume different roles such as caregiver, play mate and narrator, or if the child is older they can be an adviser or mentor. The most intensive relationship appears to be present with the maternal grandmother. Ambivalent or negative reviews of grandparents were very seldom seen in the study, and if so they relate to isolated cases.

And how does it look from the grandparents' side: 90 per cent of responding grandmothers felt joy, pride and enrichment through their grandchildren. The German psychotherapist and educationalist Harald Uhlendorff describes this in a large, representative-scale study (Uhlendorff, 2003). The grandchildren gave the grandmothers the feeling of staying young and being needed. Over 70 per cent found that being a grandmother is even more beautiful than motherhood, mainly because they did not have to raise the grandchildren. Women found with grandchildren once more a – socially recognized – role and an identity as a grandmother.

In Swiss and German studies the grandparent–grandchild relationship has a positive role. This is not only the case in these countries. Even in the United States, where a large number of studies on this subject have been published, there is a similar view.

Several studies point out, for example, that the health of grandparents is impaired when they lose contact with their grandchildren; for example, when the parents separate, divorce or move away. An American study that used the data from a longitudinal-sectional study of generations ('The Longitudinal Study of Generations'; it began in 1971 as a study of 2,044 participants from 328 three-generation families) examined the emotional health of grandparents who lost contact with grandchildren due to an event such as divorce, moving, etc., with those who had not lost them. This group experienced a steeper increase in depressive symptoms compared with other grandparents. However, the depressive symptoms went away after three years and the grandparents returned to an inner balance (Drew & Silverstein, 2007).

Other studies were occupied with the changing importance of grandparents when the children get older. Already in Höpflinger's studies it was clear that adolescent grandchildren no longer share all of their experiences and thoughts with their grandparents. In an American study the importance of grandparents has been examined from the perspective of 4–5-year-old, 8–9-year-old and 11–12-year-old children. There were significant differences in the quality of perception between the age groups. Small children valued grandparents for their indulgence and patience, the middle group loved the fun-making activities with the grandparents and the oldest group broached the issue of the distance to their grandparents. The study concludes that one must take into account the changing needs of ageing grandchildren when it comes to the importance of grandparents. The researchers suggest that the changing importance grandparents have for pubescent children might be something to do with the grandparents becoming older and frailer and that pubescent teenagers begin to be more interested in their peers (Kahana & Kahana, 1970).

In a classic piece of literature on grandparents, four symbolic functions of grandparents are listed:

1   Grandparents symbolize the fact of simply being there. They indicate the intergenerational continuity.
2   They are the 'guardians of the family', who pay attention to the observance of the intergenerational values of the tribe.
3   They work as a 'referee' when it comes to negotiations regarding intergenerational continuity within the family.
4   They are figures within the social construction of the biography of younger family members. They give and interpret meaning as far as the personal past is concerned (Bengtson, 1985, p. 25).

In summary, it can be said that already this small overview shows the importance of the specific relationship between grandparents and grandchildren. However, I would like to add that the growth of research does not necessarily mean that the relationship between the two was formerly less important. The relationship probably always had its place in the family structure. In earlier centuries, people lived closer together; for example, in a farmhouse in which several generations lived there would generally have been less mobility. Even today children in many African and Caribbean countries live with their grandparents, partly because the parents are at work in a distant city or in another country, partly because of parental illness. Grandparents were probably always a back-up for parents. However, it seems that with the increasing number of women with careers and the longer lives of grandparents, the time that the grandparents spend together with grandchildren is growing strongly.

A note about African cultures: in these cultures, grandparents always lived closer to the family and are seen as the embodiment of the past and the ones with the greatest knowledge of family stories. They tell these verbally to their grandchildren, thereby providing moral values, and are considered general consultants and leaders of the boys. Grandparents are considered wise because they have lived longer than the others, they retain the collective memory of a society. Traditionally the elderly in Africa have been highly valued, but this is nevertheless subject to change caused by European colonialism, Americanization, urbanization and expansion of Western values, which have undermined their position (Adjaye & Aborampah, 2004; Mbele, 2004).

I agree with Simone de Beauvoir, who examined the status of the elderly in different cultures and concluded that the elderly have a place either at the top or at the bottom of the social ladder. The elderly who have eminence are cultishly worshipped. On the other hand, there are cultures in which the elderly are looked upon as useless eaters (de Beauvoir, 1997). These different perspectives are familiar in many cultures: 'Sheikh' was in pre-Islamic Arabia an honorific title and means 'old man' (Volkmann, 2000, p. 112). As people became older they were in many cultures given respect and reverence. In some tribes the salutation of grandmother or grandfather was used to show respect to the elders, regardless of whether they were blood relatives or not, because they had ancient knowledge and were near to ancient spirit forces. Older people offer a tribal consciousness, roots and a strong hold. On the other hand, in European countries there is prejudice against the elderly and the term 'age discrimination' points to a certain devaluation of age. This does not include, interestingly enough, the grandparent–grandchild relationship. Höpflinger explains, as noted earlier, that the grandparent role is one of the few positive age roles, while old age would otherwise be devalued (Höpflinger et al., 2006).

An interesting study of the American family by therapists Robert Beland and Terry Mills shows the positive and negative images of grandparents in children's literature since 1984. Sixty-four books that contain grandparents were analysed, with the result that almost only positive pictures were found. Grandparents were described 95 per cent of the time as independent, happy, wise and understanding. Only 3 per cent received a negative rating. They have been described positively, even if they are sick – for example, have Alzheimer's or have lost their memory. Even when they were carried off by death, the stories described a positive effect on the family, such that all family members recalled the grandparent and dug up positive stories with a result that the family ties became stronger (Beland & Mills, 2001). It might be that these stories also had a moral impetus. Nevertheless: the fact remains that people of grandparent-age often become milder and more peaceful, and the chance is greater that grandchildren can have more positive experiences with them than their parents did.

Developmental considerations of the grandparent– grandchild relationship

Many social scientists emphasize that the age of the grandchild plays an important role when it comes to the importance of the grandparent–grandchild relationship. As young people enter puberty they tend to not be as interested in their grandparents as they once were (Höpflinger *et al.*, 2006; Kahana & Kahana, 1970). From a developmental point of view, the same is assumed. There are too few investigations, so the subject will only be touched upon here.

The Jungian Joanne Wieland-Burston from Munich suspects that early grandchild–grandparent relationships consist of idealizations: young grandchildren idealize grandparents because they know everything; grandparents idealize their grandchildren because they embody life and vibrancy. They also happily accept the grandchild's idealization in a situation in which they no longer feel as strong and agile (Wieland-Burston, 2010). The grandson, as the songwriter Tinu Heiniger describes in the above song, commands the patient grandfather to do what he wants. As grandparents often no longer work and do not have to raise children, their approach with the grandchild is different; they fulfil the grandchild's 'instructions' and thus strengthen their self-efficacy (Knox, 2012). This occurs even if the grandson has to explain to the grandmother how the phone or the computer works. The relationship is more relaxed, possibly pampering; both tend to reinforce each other. This can strengthen the mutual 'grandiose' and intimate relationship (see also the 'Heidi' story).

Grandparents introduce the children to the family history, to their ethical and religious values, attitudes, rituals or festivals; they may tell stories of the past and look at photo albums together. This gives a grandchild a vertical dimension of identity, as the psychoanalyst Peter Schwob explains (Schwob, 1988, 1990). It is insightful that the self-esteem and self-efficacy feeling of a human being has to do with its own history, with his parents, grandparents and generally with his ancestors. The sense of identity (like the family feeling) of a human being increases when he feels part of a tribe.

The relationship with grandparents is very important for neglected, exploited or abused children, who sometimes find stability, warmth and acceptance with grandparents – if that relationship is not influenced by negative experiences such as shame, injury or betrayal. The studies from Switzerland, Germany and the United States show that the grandparent–grandchild relationship is rated positively by a large majority. This is interesting because while parents complain about a negative relationship with their parents in childhood, their children often in turn have a good relationship with them. This is an empirical fact that one often encounters in psychotherapy and analysis.

The idealizing tendency changes when the grandchildren are older: in various studies it is mentioned that the topic of sexuality is omitted from the grandparent–grandchild relationship (e.g. Höpflinger *et al.*, 2006). It can therefore be assumed that no oedipal rivalry occurs and that sexuality is kept secret from the grandparents. With sexual maturity, it seems that the relationship comes to a natural end (as is clearly visible in the fairy tale *Little Red Riding Hood*).

However, the German psychoanalyst Peter Schwob argues that grandparents have a special meaning in the transitional time. He postulates the concept of 'quadrangulation' (Schwob, 1988): grandparents are the fourth party in the relationship of father–mother–child by analogy with the function of 'triangulation' with the father in relation to the mother–child relationship. Triangulation means that the father as the third party comes into the dyad between mother and child and helps the child to resolve the symbiotic dyad. This is analogous with the grandparent. They could help the grandchild to break away from the parents. At the same time, their presence means that this does not mean the dissolution of family bonds. Grandparents could serve the children as transitional objects, which allows them to distance themselves gradually and become more independent.

Normally, outsiders such as pop idols, teachers or other young individuals help them to gradually better distance themselves from their parents. But grandparents have a special status as they are the parents of the parents. They are close and yet clearly separated. Therefore, it is easy for even young children to experience them as a representative of the parents. But when they get older, grandparents can also act as a substitute, especially if the young person has a strong negative attitude towards the parents, according to Schwob. Grandparents can have a moderating influence on parents when they exaggerate (Schwob, 1990). On the other hand, the American gerontologist E.M. Timberlake found that grandparents do not exercise much power in those societies where they are very close to the grandchildren (Timberlake, 1980). In addition, it must be added that there probably are countries in which grandparents alongside parents form a common front against rebellious children (e.g. possibly in Balkan countries or Turkey).

Schwob summarizes that grandparents can help kids who have ambivalent relationships with their parents just by being there, and do not themselves have any child-rearing intentions. They know that the parents were also children and once even went through puberty, too. They can help the grandchild to make a more mature, realistic assessment (Schwob, 1988, 1990).

The relationship between grandchild and grandparent will change again when the grandparents are old and weak, and when they eventually die. As they age, the grandchildren see how their muscles become weaker, their memory becomes worse, their eyes grow weaker, the skin is wrinkled, the figure bent. The grandparents need aids such as walking sticks; the parents need to help them. Grandchildren learn that there are illnesses and finally death. This existential experience leaves no one untouched. The fairy tale researcher Gertrud Ennulat writes in the book *Alter und Weisheit in Märchen* (Age and Wisdom in Fairy Tales) about a grandchild who spoke with his grandmother about her impending death. There arose an awkward pause after this question, a pause 'in which a little fear was spreading, suddenly the child looked at the grandmother with different eyes' (Ennulat, 2000, p. 84).

Wieland-Burston mentions that with the ageing of the grandparents, grandchildren are faced with the existential issues of disease, decay and death. Often it is the first death that the grandchildren experience, and the question of where the grandparents have gone is in the room and must be dealt with. When the grandparent actually dies, the familiar rituals follow. Grandchildren experience these rituals, and they see how their family deals with a dead person, they see the tears, the pain and sorrow of parents and relatives, the funeral home, the burial and the wake. Wieland-Burston argues that death can be understood as a (first) separation experience. The idealization finally stops here if it has not already happened (Wieland-Burston, 2010). This archetypal process of parting from a formerly important person is also reflected in fairy tales, such as *Little Red Riding Hood* (see the previous chapter).

In summary, it can be said that the developmental issues of attachment, identity/rootedness and detachment/separation occur in the grandparent–grandchild relationship and shape the identity of a grandchild.

Part II

Clinical section

Chapter 7

Intersubjectivity in clinical practice

The previous chapter clearly shows how intersubjective processes can characterize interpersonal relationships and how archetypal images may appear. This also applies to therapeutic work. The work with clients is also characterized by intersubjective processes. Even though internal working models or the involved people's complexes structure the encounter, on the other hand something completely new can occur – for example, when an archetypal moment of meeting or a present moment happens. The possibility of this should always be left open, e.g. in therapy the subject of grandparents can occur suddenly and gain an influence that one would not initially suspect.

An encounter in the therapeutic situation depends on whether the two parties have a common meaning for what happens, whether they jointly understand something or jointly share an emotional experience. An interpretation alone does not create an encounter. The meaning does not have to be verbalized, it does not have to be deliberate, it can appear as an emergent phenomenon in which the existing could be put in context and 'understood'. (Daniel Stern and his Boston Group would describe these phenomena as moments of meeting.) The understanding of the meaning of what happened can be disturbed, you do not really understand the other, talk it over and thus nothing is 'left'. A moment of meeting is thus not possible.

But what makes encounter possible? Perhaps we first need to know about the interactions in therapy.

Interactions in the therapeutic situation

The American psychoanalyst Frank Lachmann has examined interactions in more detail and propagated three principles that he found in analysis and therapy with an intersubjective perspective (Lachmann, 2008):

1 *Interactive and self-regulation*: each partner causes something in the other and constantly regulates his own state; for example, his emotions and inner turmoil. Self-regulation can be maintained during periods of tension, and in times of frustration a sense of security and stability. This is done through words, but also through body language, tone, rhythm of speech and expressions of empathic understanding. Both types transform the analytic atmosphere.

2 *Disruption and repair*: there are always breaks and pauses in an interaction; if, for example, a partner doesn't react empathically enough or has a deadpan face, the other may no longer understand. Both can repair the disruption or let it be.

3 *Emergence of strong feelings that suddenly change the atmosphere*: Lachmann mentioned the famous example of Kohut (1966) when he suddenly said to a young medical student that he was a complete idiot. This sudden outburst had been meant ironically and left no traumatic effect on the students. Every analyst knows such situations, says Lachmann, in which both have a good laugh, you really do not know why you have made such a comment and what could have led to it that one later finds themselves on a new, non-verbal and implicit level.

Lachmann discussed these three phenomenological possibilities and how he sees this interaction.

Daniel Stern (2004) also commented on interactions in a therapeutic situation. He argued that both parties feel their way forward through relational steps in therapy together. The results of the inaccuracy have emergent properties that develop two psyches from the almost similar articles. Islands of intentional consistency are generated from the uncertainty:

> These then coalesced through the same process of utilizing the potential creativity of sloppiness to forge larger spaces of shared implicit relational knowing.... It is important to emphasize that sloppiness is potentially creative only when it occurs within a well-established framework. Without that, it is only disorder.
>
> (Stern, 2004, p. 164)

There is creativity in sloppiness, to Stern, with regard to the theory of dynamical systems. He describes five different processes in a therapy:

1 Processes with sudden dramatic, therapeutic changes.

2 Negative therapeutic implications, because the opportunity for change was missed.

3   Progressive implicit change in the therapeutic relationship that sup-
    ports the desired change.
4   Processes that prepare the way for new explorations of the explicit
    material.
5   Processes which prepare the way for interpretations (Stern, 2004,
    pp. 165–184).

Both Lachmann and Stern agree that it is noticeable that the role of the
analyst is no longer indispensable for the interaction process. The subjectivity of the client, as well as the analyst, countertransference and
transmission, internal working models, complex and the potential of
archetypal images from both as well as unconscious synchronization are
the raw material of the therapeutic container. It occurs in the above interactions, as well as interpretations, theory and analytical attitude of the
therapist conducting the therapy. These are of course only approximations. What exactly happens in a therapeutic field is describable only in
approximations.

The role of the analyst

Now what is the role of the analyst in such events? As noted, psychoanalysts argue that in an intersubjective approach (and others too) that the
subjectivity of the analyst decisively influences the therapeutic situation.
An interpretation or countertransference is not neutral (Orange, 2004).
The French Jungian who created the concept of 'The transferential
chimera', François Martin-Vallas, had a similar argument. Transference
must be considered as a hybrid, a chimera. The term shows

> how the affective plane of the relationship can be supple, complex
> and nuanced, enabling energy to circulate sufficiently freely between
> the different levels of the transference so that the processes of de-
> integration and re-integration which enliven it can proceed without
> too much disturbance. Here we have, it seems to me, a real transfer-
> ential self, by which I mean a shared space, where the whole poten-
> tial of the analytic experience can be played out.
>
> (Martin-Vallas, 2006, p. 639)

In a theoretical extension of the concept of transferential chimera,
Martin-Vallas supports Jung's statement that doctor and patient
find themselves in a relationship, whose origin existed in their mutual

unconscious (Jung, 1946, §364). That was a key point, because this statement implies that 'the countertransference as being essential for the proper conduct of the transference; this would confirm the notion that the transference and the countertransference unite to provide one of the containers for the transference' (Martin-Vallas, 2008, p. 50). Martin-Vallas believes that there are more containers, but one of them appears to be the countertransference and transmission, in which the process can unfold in a secure framework.

C.G. Jung and the role of the analyst

Martin-Vallas refers in his comments to C.G. Jung, who in various parts of his oeuvre repeatedly includes the role of the analyst, as he pointed out in volume 16, especially in its first part, 'Problems of Modern Psychotherapy' (1929) and 'Principles of Practical Psychotherapy' (1935), as well as in the second part of the 'Psychology of the Transference' (1946) and the mutual interdependence and influence of analyst and client. While many of his remarks seem intuitive, one can nevertheless see them as the forerunner of the intersubjectivity theory (Otscheret, 2005).

In 1929 he published an article in the Swiss Medical Yearbook on 'Problems of Modern Psychotherapy', in which he pointed out the countertransference and emphasized it as a means of knowledge of the physician in the analysis:

> For two personalities to meet is like mixing two different chemical substances: if there is any combination at all, both are transformed. In any effective psychological treatment, the doctor is bound to influence the patient; but this influence can only take place if the patient has a reciprocal influence on the doctor. You can exert no influence if you are not susceptible to influence. It is futile for the doctor to shield himself from the influence of the patient and to surround himself with a smokescreen of fatherly and professional authority. By so doing he only denies himself the use of a highly important organ of information. The patient influences him unconsciously none the less, and brings about changes in the doctor's unconscious which are well known to many psychotherapists.... One of the best known symptoms of this kind is the counter-transference evoked by the transference.
>
> (Jung, 1929, §163)

In particular, in the article 'Psychology of the Transference' (Jung, 1946), Jung systematized the transference on the basis of alchemical ideas. It lacks a theoretical basis, but certain systematization (perhaps even too much systematization) is available from Jung. In his view, not only the consciousness of the therapist and client influence each other, but also their unconscious and namely mutually, intrapsychically as interpersonally, so six possibilities of mutual interference are present in the therapeutic field.

Therefore, the unconscious from both are important because in the view of analytical psychology psychological contents are projected mutually, especially if they are unconscious. The projections are important in order to be able to detect any unconscious material.

Within the therapeutic space transference and countertransference can be established and contain unconscious material. The result is a third factor in the therapeutic space (the 'transferential chimera'; Martin-Vallas) or in Jung's words:

> The elusive, deceptive, ever-changing content that possesses the patient like a demon now flits about from patient to doctor and, as the third party in the alliance, continues its game, sometimes impish and teasing, sometimes really diabolical. The alchemists aptly personified it as the wily god of revelation Hermes or Mercurius
>
> (Jung, 1946, §384)

The third party in the therapy, *Mercurius*, according to Jung, is once independent, but once permeated by mutual projections from doctor and patient. Jung has not clearly expressed this. It is the question of whether the 'third party', this Mercurius, has more to do with the patient or more with the relationship between analyst and patient.

The Jungian Lilian Otscheret thinks this intersubjective third party from Jung only deals with the patient. She criticizes that the intersubjective third does not have any connection to the other. Jung knows only *one* inner subjective third party, namely the transcendent function that arises when the I is found in an unsolvable tension and is open for a contradictory meditative symbol that shows the way from 'either–or' to a synthesis of opposing elements.

What does Otschert mean with the transcendent function? In order to generally understand Jung's reference to a third for therapeutic exchange processes, it will be briefly referred to as the transcendent function: Jung wrote in 1916 in the article 'The transcendent function' about the relationship of consciousness to the unconscious, especially about the one-sided consciousness, that then builds an energetic compensatory tension in the unconscious (Jung, 1916):

> The *counter-position* in the unconscious is not dangerous so long as it does not possess any high energy-value. But if the tension increases as a result of too great one-sidedness the counter-tendency breaks through into consciousness, usually just at the moment when it is most important to maintain the conscious direction. Thus the speaker makes a slip of the tongue just when he particularly wishes not to say anything stupid.
>
> (Jung, 1916, §138)

Jung saw the unconscious and consciousness as two complementary halves of something whole. If the consciousness is too unilateral then the unconscious reacts. If one is in the consciousness, for example, always good-natured and wants to please everyone, a tension builds up in the unconscious and you may respond ruthlessly. Jung further argued: 'The tendencies of the unconscious and of the consciousness are the two factors that together make up the transcendent function' (Jung, 1916, §145). The task of the analyst is to mediate the transcendental function to the patient, i.e. 'helps him to bring conscious and unconscious together and so arrive at a new attitude' (Jung, 1916, §146).

We need the unconscious as a complement to consciousness, otherwise we are only half human. The contact with the unconscious should therefore be flexible; we should remain open to the voice of the unconscious, as seen in dreams, for example. If the unconscious reaction is suppressed or drifts away from consciousness that is how it loses the regulatory influence. The result may be, for example, an instinct loss, an impoverishment of consciousness, a dull, diffused discomfort, a kind of boredom, disgust, exhaustion of consciousness, all faults that cause people to seek therapy. The responsibility of the physician, therefore, is to help the patient so that he can maintain a balance of consciousness and the unconscious using the transcendent function – for example, a symbol appears that helps both to reconnect with each other.

Otscheret refers to this transcendental function that creates the 'third' as a mediating symbol which represents a third factor, a third position that does not exist in the field of logic. Through the action of the transcendent function, the unconscious and archetypal fantasies came through symbols to life. However, Otscheret criticizes that the transcendental function only mediates intrapsychically between the opposites of the patient, but in a relationship with a You (Otscheret, 2005, p. 70).

It should be added that Jung developed 'The transcendent function' in 1916, whereas the 'Psychology of the transference' (1946) is one of his later works. It is possible that he saw the client only as an object attempting to balance the intrapsychic tension by the transcendent function, whereby the analyst only helps and thus there is no contact with others. But I imagine that he also looked in later years at the object as a subject, that meets a subject and that Jung later implemented this intersubjective turn. Otherwise his numerous observations, particularly in the 'Psychology of the transference' about the exchange processes in the therapy cannot be understood.

Partial psyches of clients

In clinical work, in addition to intersubjective processes, there is always the possibility that internal working models and clients' complexes appear and are projected in experience with relevant others. This is also the case for the therapist, who should have learnt this during their training. We all carry within us a *number* of such working models and complexes, as we have various experiences, with the mother, with the teacher or with the grandmother. The Jungian Jean Knox goes so far as to speak of 'multiple selves' which arise – depending on the experience of the self-with-others and internalizing these relationship patterns. According to her, there is no unifying centre of consciousness or unconscious, but diverse selves, each of which may be in focus depending on the context (Knox, 2012, p. 455).

In other words: depending on the situation in a therapy, different partial psyches of a client can emerge. This partial psyches can be different for the grandparent memories as compared to the parent memories, especially when no nourishing experiences were available at the parental level but were at the grandparent level which could stimulate the child's sense of self-agency, in the sense of turn-taking, namely to have the feeling that I exist. Archetypal expectations might have been differently fulfilled and stored in implicit memory. The resulting partial psyches don't have to be connected in the psyche but can be dissociated.

In addition, it is not only the past experiences that play a role, but also the present – for example, the moment when therapy starts. The fact that a client usually goes into therapy in a crisis situation makes it more possible for the emergence of archetypal images. Clients cannot carry on with their existing possibilities and strategies and are faced with hurdles and obstacles, with feelings of helplessness, hopelessness and instability. That makes them go to therapy. As François Martin-Vallas rightly observed, you hardly feel the archetypes in times of stability. They appear in times of instability, when everything is in chaos, when you are unsure and when the right environmental conditions such as pressure and temperature are available (Martin-Vallas, 2013). The readiness for allowing archetypal images is therefore greater in a crisis situation.

The client's sense of self is at the beginning and during therapy often open to certain changes. The purpose of therapy is to remove inadequate internal working models and complexes and to create new experiences and new internal working models. Likewise, a hitherto suppressed development process should be possible through other mental structures as an archetypal image. The behaviour of 'Heidi', for example, triggered such a development process in the old man.

Knox even thinks that the therapeutic relationship triggers an unconscious expectation pattern of future interpersonal experiences (Knox, 2003, p. 201). A lot occurs already *before* the first hour as *in* the first hour with the analyst. Hopes and expectations are awakening, expectations as Knox thinks, to have more self-agency, which is the basis of the sense of self. According to Knox, self-agency involves the experience that we can influence our physical and relational environment, that our actions and intentions have an effect on the people around us and cause a reaction with them; this experience of action and result creates in all disciplines the core of the definition of effectiveness and forms the basis for the sense of self (Knox, 2012, p. 454).

Thus, the therapeutic vessel holds much in itself: expectations, hopes and unconscious activation willingness of working models, complexes and archetypal images of both. In this event it is the job of the analyst to initiate processes of development. Various means are available to him.

Theory, technique and interpretation versus intersubjectivity

Psychoanalysts, as well as analytical psychologists, according to C.G. Jung, have a set of interventions, including their knowledge, the technology, the interpretation, the analytic attitude, the symbolic attitude or what today is understood as intersubjective attitude. Within the Jungian debate a controversy arose where a more post-Kleinian Jungian debated with a more intersubjective Jungian.

Thus, the English post-Kleinian and Jungian William Meredith-Owen disputes critically the ideas of the American relational psychoanalyst Jessica Benjamin (in the USA they do not speak of intersubjectivity, but of relational psychoanalysis), who is known as one of the founders of the theory of intersubjectivity. Meredith-Owen criticizes her approach as well as the conception of the Jungian Warren Colman, who picked up the ideas of the intersubjective (Meredith-Owen, 2013).

It must be added that Jessica Benjamin accused the post-Kleinian of bringing the theory before the experience in the analytical space. Benjamin argued that such an analyst takes a dissociated observational stance and compares the transference of the client with the theory, which then would be a barrier for a more healing empathy. The wounded part of the patient feels thereby re-traumatized because it will become part of a theory. The patient feels excluded (Benjamin, 2004).

Colman argues along the same lines. Let us listen to him: Colman describes a case of a young man who developed a strong father–son transference–countertransference from the beginning (Colman, 2013). The patient spoke in a session about the stress of his job in social services in which he was struggling with budget cuts and political pressure. The patient regretted that he did not dare to talk about the pressure in a meeting with his superiors. He felt that he was rebelling against the norms of the ruthless business-oriented world of his father and wondered how he should now react. Colman adds, for the reader, that he had been exposed to similar pressure in his earlier career and that he could therefore empathize well. He manifested spontaneously towards the client: 'Don't let the bastards grind you down'.

Colman writes that he knew that he had responded to him as he would to his own son. He had expressed his own values and beliefs that were implicitly the opposite of the values of the client's father. He, however, felt that it was perhaps even more important that he gave the client fatherly advice, since his father never took the time or effort to talk to him in this way. In retrospect, Colman thinks, the patient had gotten an answer from him that was consistent with his feelings and his willingness to share something about himself; maybe it was the most valuable thing, mainly because it was unusual. He had thus implicitly confirmed the client's need for a paternal relationship in which one mutually identifies themselves (Colman, 2013, p. 210).

Meredith-Owen is opposed to this notion of 'mutual identification'. He says he is uncomfortable with this term, as if there were an underlying assumption of the value of experience of seamless matches in therapy.

Colman made it clear that he had only described a specific reaction with a certain patient, and that he was aware of the pressure of going in the direction of enactments. However, Colman thinks, a more neutral attitude that could be interpreted as the wish of the client to have paternal support, could have missed the 'moment of meeting' and reinforced the old, repetitive deprivation of the client. Such an interpretation from the abstinent analyst could have caused negative father transference according to Colman.

Meredith-Owen complains that the emergence of common feelings is more important than cognitive differentiation. Reckless father-projections would thereby be enhanced rather than modified and the personal ruthlessness remains split. If you want to achieve a 'moment of meeting', the possible dark side that arises is that you subtly move away from a workgroup to a 'gang' (in Bion's terminology). Vital but painful parts of the psychic reality remain split and projected if one creates the illusion of an exclusive relationship between the analyst and the patient. That is not a basis for a truly soothing experience, says Meredith-Owen. But the relational therapist presents such scenarios as if there was only one option, namely 'instead of'. There would be no 'as well as' within the meaning of the oedipal triangle of parent–child in which the parents have a relationship with themselves as well as with the child – or, applied to analysis, the analyst has a relationship with the client, but also with the 'third' in the room. For Meredith-Owen it is not clear why an interpretation that sensitively recognizes the repeated deprivation of clients could not have led to a 'moment of meeting' (Meredith-Owen, 2013).

Meredith-Owen thinks that the analytical goal is to reach the triangulation and a symbolic area. For this he uses the interpretation which should cause something in the client's psyche. Of course, a client also needs an empathic acknowledgement so that a basis is created on which the rigours of the triangulation can continuously survive. The more regressive a patient is, the more Meredith-Owen would agree with Colman. It does not appear, however, as if he makes such technical considerations, but rather tosses them aside because Colman says: 'The idea that the analysis is more defined by the analyst's attitude than their theory or technique is borne out by research evidence that shows good outcomes for psychotherapy to be independent of theoretical perspective' (Colman, 2013, p. 213).

Meredith-Owen replies that outcomes research and its evidence is somewhat diffuse and mouldable. What bothers him is the claim that the attitude of the analyst is viewed as something that is separate from theory and technique. Therein lies the essence of analytic perspective, namely that they integrate all three (relationship, theory and technique), and that constitutes the aesthetic power of the work (Meltzer & Harris Williams, 1988). In his clinical experience, there was nothing more touching and more effective than clinical moments in which the analytical attitude can combine deep symbolic structures with transference dynamics. 'This is the hard won heart of the analysis: and it is vulnerable to erosion by the seductive warmth of relational promise' (Meredith-Owen, 2013, p. 607) Meredith-Owen proposes instead to delve deeper into the countertransference as Jung suggested with his gate model of transference (Jung, 1946). Jung's contribution, with his innovative insight into the exchange of the analysand's unconscious with the analyst, may well anticipate relational 'co-construction'. The theory appeared not to be an obstacle.

Of course, the balance between the analyst and the client's mood and rhythm is a central task. Central is also providing an analytical field in which tone, intonation, facial expressions and gestures of the client and his narratives are empathically understood and accepted by the therapist. But that alone is not enough in my eyes. I agree with Meredith-Owen, that it is not the sole task of the analyst to establish a mutual unconscious synchronization with the patient and to be a mere resonating body (Roesler, 2013). Theory, technique and interpretation are all instruments of the analyst, if not additionally like the analytical attitude, the symbolic setting and the production of a third, including the maintenance of a tension that is central to the analytic aesthetics. Otherwise there is the danger of unconscious enactments and acting out of feelings that are based on complexes of the analyst.

The transference always constellates in a fluctuating and complex relationship situation: it can be understood to a certain degree but that's it. Expressions of feeling and acting out of feelings may be important aspects at times, but we cannot thereby heal old wounds completely.

Chapter 8

Clinical examples

Sandra and the Rapunzel-grandmother

The 32-year-old patient, let's call her Sandra, opted for psychotherapy, as she had an abortion in the eighth week of pregnancy a few months earlier and was very sad about this loss. Her life seemed to stand still; she was depressed and could not decide which way her life should go, professionally or relationally. Everything was questioned: the profession, the marriage, and herself. She was in a deep crisis.

Opposite me sat a slim, smartly dressed young woman. She sat down sideways so she could not look at me without turning her head. When she turned, she looked with wide eyes but didn't really see me. She spoke haltingly, more to herself, and complained about the unborn child that she had wanted so much. Her posture was insecure and inhibited. I asked about other feelings. She said: 'I am confused, I can't understand why such a thing could happen'. The relationship with her husband was presently distant; he understood her grief, but did not understand why she was still blocked and why she now also doubted her work and the relationship. They often had disputes; his opinion was life goes on. She felt guilty towards him because on the one hand she knew he was right, but on the other hand she was paralysed.

Her gynaecologist advised her not to wait too long to get pregnant again. However, the client did not dare to try. She didn't understand her behaviour, why she had slipped into this fundamental crisis; she looked again and again absently out of the window during the first session, as if she were cocooned in her own world – sad, depressed and not understanding herself.

The anamnesis revealed that her grandmother had given birth to the mother under harsh and poor conditions on a farm. The grandparents were fighting for survival, there had been epidemics among their livestock and they often worked late into the night to feed their numerous children. The grandfather died early due to a stroke, so the grandmother had to raise the children alone. The older siblings helped her as much as they could. The mother herself was one of the younger siblings. She constantly suffered under the fear that the family would be torn apart, and she felt ashamed when the village children picked on her and laughed at her shabby clothes. Sandra told this story with a detached tone, as if everything, as said, were wrapped in a cocoon.

Her mother married early and gave birth to three children, a girl and two boys. In the former boom-time both parents worked a lot to become moderately prosperous and have a secure income. Therefore, they asked the grandmother to watch the kids while they went to work. The two brothers were extraverted, active and sporty children, much to the delight of the grandmother. Sandra, however, developed into an introverted child who was prone to daydreaming and preferred playing with dolls. The grandmother and the mother had always turned up their noses when she took out the dolls, she said. She looked at me for the first time as if for confirmation that this was okay. I nodded and asked: 'What was wrong with that?' She turned away again and answered: 'My grandmother was convinced that life is a struggle that we must be tough, otherwise we do not survive. They often said to us, "If you knew what I have suffered, you would not play so happy."'

For a moment this phrase hung in the air. The question crossed my mind of whether the grandmother had been envious of the joy of the children and whether there existed a connection with the crisis situation in any form. It was a hypothesis. Apart from that I didn't succeed in establishing an emotional contact with her in the initial consultation.

We agreed weekly meetings with the goal of processing the miscarriage and a clarification of the professional and relational perspectives. From then on, the patient came regularly and on time to the sessions. As first diagnostic clues I noted weak self-esteem, a lack of autonomous development, dissociative defences and a depressive processing mode. In Jungian terminology it should be added that her persona – her role and adaption to the outside – was rigid and had now cracked. Her ego strength was only weakly developed, while aggression, creativity and imagination were in the shadow. I also suspected a negative transference because of her internal working models and complex, since she refused contact and was unconsciously afraid that I might react like the grandmother or mother. In the countertransference I realized a slight disinterest in me and a rather unusual wish to look at her problems from a purely objective perspective. Negative projections on other relevant people were probably also to be found, and that meant she was maintaining her dissociative mechanisms.

In the subsequent meetings she spoke about her distant relationship with her father. She had hardly seen him in her childhood as he was often absent. Her relationship with her mother was distant. Her mother held on to the strong grandmother, who had the budget under control. The patient said she had suffered much from her: 'She constantly criticized me when I was dreaming instead of doing my homework. I made up stories in which I was a princess and that made her very angry', lamented Sandra.

In the following I will focus on the influence and effect of the grandmother on Sandra. This will inevitably neglect other important influences by the parents and especially by the father. The relationship between the grandmother and Sandra was crucial for Sandra's later development, which is why I now concentrate on this.

A fragmentary excerpt from a session shows the following relationship. As usual, Sandra came to the session on time. She looked like always – a little absent – and told me of her fear of the eyes of the grandmother, who looked hard and angry. She told me of her fear of her voice, the screaming nagging – she wastes her time, she should not be dreaming, but do her homework. Sandra said that this screaming unsettled her very much because she always had the feeling that something was wrong with her. She was just paralysed, looking down, waiting for the attacks to finish, but would have liked to fall into the ground, so bad, so useless and worthless she had felt. She did not look at me during the story; her figure was slumped. I could empathize with her panic and paralysis, on the one hand, but at the same time had also the desire to tell her that she should fight back and stand up for herself. I didn't verbalize this countertransference feeling. There was a crippling, relentless mood in the room; time seemed to stand still. The power of the archetype of the evil witch was for noticeable to us both; this power was now in the room, but not yet named.

The client added, after a while: 'I envied my brothers, who had no problems with her'. Her mother supported the grandmother, not the client:

> Bad for me were that she told me in secret, she sees herself in me. She did not say anything further, but today I think my mother was too weak against the fierce grandmother. I am disappointed about her. I would have liked more maternal support for the attacks. In the

world of grandmother, you had to just work, otherwise there was nothing, no feelings, no daydreams, I could not think up spinning stories.

The grandmother's power was enhanced by the accommodating mother and the absent father. The mother suppressed her feelings and offered no role model with regard to expressions of feelings for her daughter.

The atmosphere was marked by a helpless, paralysing feeling, which was hard to endure – even for me – and not to act. Sandra fled earlier, and even now, in the defence mechanism of dissociation to survive in the face of fears triggered by the grandmother. The archetypal image of Rapunzel occurred in me. The witch appeared to destroy the autonomy of the girl and kept her far away, trapped in a tower. The picture helped me to better understand. The witch in the fairy tale *Rapunzel* was childless and held Rapunzel captive due to her envy, so that she could not live independently. Applied to Sandra's biography, this meant that the grandmother was destructive and envious as the witch, by stalling the creative and imaginative characteristics of the patient. There were features she could not live herself. She trapped the patient in the tower, which is also a symbol for the dissociation tendencies of the patient – to be inaccessible for emotions and creativity.

Let us recall Fraiburg's 'ghosts in the nursery' (Fraiburg *et al.*, 1975), where she mentioned the unconscious disclosure of repressed feelings: parents or grandparents do not only educate, but unconsciously pass on in education the contents of unremembered previous relationship experiences of fear and helplessness. Traumas are passed on from generation to generation if they are not experienced and verbalized.

In this debilitating therapeutic situation Sandra began to see what was bothering her: the grandmother had stalled their creative parts. In the countertransference I no longer realized only a critical attitude, but now also a compassionate response. She was sad and touching. She described that she had learned a profession that the parents and the grandmother had persuaded her to follow and which promised security and material prosperity. Her thoughts and imagination had been narrowed at the time of choosing a career, so she agreed. From today's perspective the dry, logical world of her profession is too desolate.

The complex, which grew out of the intense relationship with the grandmother, was a tough, unforgiving attitude towards her. Just as the grandmother had treated Sandra, so Sandra treated herself, with the effect that she became depressed. Her guilt was overwhelming as she unconsciously took over the debt of the grandmother not to talk about her past. Anger, sadness, shame and guilt were split, but returned unconscious in the form of depression in Sandra.

At this point I add another excerpt from a session. After one and a half years of therapy Sandra came one day happily to the session; she was pregnant again, adding at the same time that she was afraid she would lose this child also. She looked at me intently; I comforted her. There was now a resonance between us; the mood had changed compared to the beginning. The patient was more in contact with the other and open to intervention; her transference had developed in a positive direction.

She said: 'I'm afraid to lose my child; also, I feel guilty towards the deceased child. If I am happy now, then it's like I forget this and I'm not allowed. That's my problem'. I asked: 'You want to give the dead a place, so that you will not forget?' She said yes, but that is difficult; she has difficulties distinguishing between death and life. She could not look forward to something new and leave the deceased back. After a pause I asked: 'What could you do to solve this problem?' After a while she looked at me and thought she could write about it. (It should be added that we had already talked for a while about her joy in writing. The grandmother had demonized her writing because of its uselessness. The patient, however, loved to write stories and fairy tales, and did so secretly in childhood. The daydreaming and fantasizing had been a forbidden place.) We talked about the hardness of the grandmother's ban and I asked her if she did not get angry due to the ban. She looked puzzled and said, no, she does not feel anything like that.

We continued to talk about writing as a resource with which she was able to maintain the memory of the deceased child. At the end of the session she came back to the subject of anger, saying she had no right to be angry about her grandmother, criticizing me. Her grandmother would not have been responsible for the situation. A now moment emerged. The intersubjective atmosphere was now dense. The status quo of the relationship was endangered and undermined the existing intersubjective field. Should I respond authentically and honestly, or rather support her?

I opted for the confrontation because her ego strength had risen. 'Why not', I answered, 'why apologize to the grandmother? As a child you couldn't help the circumstances of your grandmother'. With that intervention I favoured a new context. Such confrontation is not always possible and old patterns can continue to prevail after a confrontation. She said nothing, but looked at me thoughtfully. I waited. Finally, she said, she feels a little anger that she had to adapt and that her family so little recognized her character. I smiled at her. The now moment turned this time into a moment of meeting.

The urge to write was so strong that she decided to abandon the profession she had taken only for her parents' and the grandmother's sake. A supportive factor was that her husband had received a job offer in Southeast Asia. The two discussed the emigration. The patient took a chance and enrolled simultaneously at a distance university, which offered training in creative writing.

Sandra had to start without useful, old forces, as did Rapunzel, but her creativity and spontaneity, which were long in the shadow, had become opportunities to be lived and realized.

Rosemarie and the witch-grandmother

A 32-year-old client, Rosemarie, was looking for treatment because of insomnia, nervousness, phobias, vague fears and depressive slumps. She seemed, in spite of these symptoms, lively, somewhat girlish and 'cool', in the sense that nothing can harm me. Her family doctor gave her the benzodiazepine Xanax, which helped her against her fears. Initially she wanted to keep the medication.

The main cause behind her symptoms was her wish for a fourth child while continuing her education. Although the three children already took a lot of her energy, she longed for another. Her basic conflict at the time of starting the treatment was harbouring many plans and ideas, but feeling exhausted and fearing she could not savour enough life.

In psychotherapy, the first urgent symptoms and complaints were dealt with. Among others, the daily intake of Xanax was problematized with the result that the patient began to reduce the intake. The patient began to stabilize somewhat.

One day she told the following story about her maternal grandmother: Her grandmother had lived in a small mountain village in Switzerland, which was located in a narrow valley where the sun disappeared already in the late afternoon behind the peaks. The grandparents lived in an old farmhouse made of wood, typical of the former construction low ceilings, high thresholds and with a room that was normally only used on Sunday when visitors came. Then the nice dishes were taken out and covered in this parlour. The mother of the client had grown up in this house. Later, the mother started in the same mountain village her own family, where

Rosemarie grew up with her three siblings. The mother visited the grand-mother with their children every Sunday.

In Rosemary's eyes these Sundays were a 'horror'; she described the following: the grandmother was always laying on the couch in the parlour. The room was kept dark. 'I already knew upon entering, that my grandmother lay on the couch and spread a bad mood. She was sick. Sure, I should have compassion, but she revolted me so much – until now. I think she faked it', huffed the client.

The anger was noticeable in our meeting, but she was more than angry, she looked shocked, angry, terrified – and trapped. Occasionally she smiled again; her expression was a mixture of anger, making fun of herself and smiling. 'This picture of lying in the dark room pursues me to date, of this silent and embittered grandmother. It appears in the most unlikely moments'. According to her description, the mood and the atmo-sphere in the room were always oppressive and claustrophobic. Time stood still, though a cuckoo clock beat loudly: tick-tock. She did not understand as a child why a clock can beat and it still feels like time stands still. She could barely endure the cramped room with the motion-less, lying grandmother.

Rosemarie sat during these visits always in the same chair, but she turned sideways so she did not have to look directly to the grandmother. After just one and a half hours – the grandmother had looked at the cuckoo clock – she walked tediously and slowly to the buffet, taking out a package of Guetsli (Swiss German for biscuits). It was always the same butter cookies that she offered the family. Rosemarie tore it always right out of her hand, which caused the grandmother to angrily say to her mother: 'Can't you educate your daughter better?' The mother each time looked guilty, but the client exulted: 'I wanted to provoke grandmother, simply because I wanted to feel a reaction or a feeling, even if it was anger. She was otherwise so seemingly dead'.

The biographical background of the grandmother showed that she had to marry a man she didn't like. Such planned marriages took place in the mountain valleys of Switzerland in those days. For this village it had pre-viously even been customary to completely seal itself off from the outside world. The 'outside' could even be the deeper valley; for many mountain people these were like 'foreign countries'. The lack of news was offset by the fact that the villagers developed fine sensoria and 'felt' when the neighbours were different to usual and greeted them in another way. Stories were recounted and recounted. Rosemarie's grandmother had this sensoria, as did the mother and herself, she said. The consequence of these fine sensoria was that there was little intimacy in the village.

Since I myself have maternal roots in a highlander family, this feeling of the foreign that frightened highlanders was not unknown. My mother had fled from the village and started a family in the city. As children we still spent our free time in the mountain village, where my parents had built a summer house (so they solved their conflicted mountain village identity versus town identity). At the beginning, at the unconscious level I suspected a fusion or match between the client and me and an implicit understanding regarding her desire to escape from the confines of the mountain valley and a preference for the anonymity of the city. After a while I rejected this hypothesis, because her situation was too different.

Rosemarie's grandmother gave birth to a crowd of children and took her role as a mother and villager very seriously, despite the planned marriage. She acquiesced in it, trying her best. First, she could indeed identify with her role. However, after a while she could no longer achieve this. She had to be operated on due to a goitre. She had been a passionate and talented singer in the village choir, but after the surgery she could no longer sing. Something had gone wrong during the operation; at least, she lost her voice. This hit her hard and she was depressed and silent and barely got out of bed. During visits she moved over to the couch. Later, she suffered painful osteoarthritis, and so became even more immobile.

The goitre operation took place at a time when Rosemary's mother reached puberty. As the youngest child, she had developed a close relationship with her mother, felt responsible for her and helped her in the household once she was bedridden. She later got a job as a shop assistant, but stayed at home when she bore children and completely took over running the household for her mother. The client described the nature of the relationship: 'My mother took my grandmother's disease very seriously. Once she told me that she still dreams, an avalanche would come and bury her mother. She must then dig her up'. In Rosemarie's description the criticism of the mother resonated: she had neglected herself and her children. The unsecure, depressed mother was not a model with which she wanted to identify.

Rosemarie grew up in this climate in the mountain village. She was already a rebellious child and freedom-loving. For as long as she could remember she wanted to escape from the small village and the close mountains. She often provoked the mother as a child, just as she did the grandmother, for the simple reason that it got a reaction. She said:

> My mother made an effort, and could not get out of misery yet. So I
> said to her always provocative: 'No.' I wanted to get her to react. I
> had the feeling that I have to save my mother. I rebelled to get
> her out.

The best was when her mother put her in her room – this was alive. Bad
was when her mother said 'I have now simply no energy left'. Then she
gave no more response. Rosemarie stood as a child often before the
mountain's dark silhouette and dreamed of how it would look
beyond them.

When the client was of age, she moved from the valley to the city. She
felt there footloose and fancy-free, and did not intend to become a mother
soon. Nevertheless, she married relatively young and gave birth to her
first child at the age of 23 years! Shortly after came two more children
for whom she must sacrifice more. She wanted to be a good mother and
put her training on hold. For a time all went well until the mentioned
symptoms emerged, and at 32 years old she wanted to start
psychotherapy.

Rosemarie developed relatively quickly a perception of her contradictory personality in psychotherapy. She was capable of introspection
and identified a freedom-loving aspect, a kind of 'hippie', a younger
woman adrift, without responsibility and who wanted to be unbound and
provoked all who wanted to stop her. On the other hand, she saw herself
as a self-sacrificing, conventional mother whose centre and content of life
were her children. Whenever the conversation turned to her hippie
personality, rage, anger and outrage emerged, especially against the
embittered grandmother, who she made responsible for the fate of her
mother. On the other hand, she was furious with herself because she was
drained, exhausted and pushed to her limits and could not accept the rebel
in her. As a sacrificing mother she was depressed and anxious, could
hardly set limits to her children and put their needs above all else.

It can be hypothetically stated that in Rosemary's portrayal a complex
is described. Complexes are defined by Jung as 'splinter psyches' (Jung,
1934a, §204). They exist separately in the unconscious, from where they
can inhibit or promote awareness at all times. Depending on the trigger in
the current situation a complex can break through, influence emotions,
cognitive representations, perceptions, expectations, fantasies, defences,
behaviour and memory contents in a way that has little to do with the
environment. The ascending complex just breaks into consciousness.
Individuals will be 'taken' from the emotional complex.

Rosemary's description suggests that her situation in the mountains, the mountain village and in particular with the grandmother had led to a complex as a splinter psyche in her personality. The complex contains the feeling and emotions of panic. Cognitively she wanted to escape, an escape into the wild, away from the confines and to become free. Likewise, distorted, generalized perceptions of limitations and a diffuse expectation of being trapped were noticed. As a protection mechanism (defence) she flew into a hippie existence, angrily provoking the environment and not taking any responsibility. The other defence was submission, in which she became a self-sacrificing, undemanding mother, fulfilling the expectations of her mother and grandmother. At the core of the complex there was the archetype of the bitter evil witch who restricted the lives of others and finally absorbed it. Due to the strength of the complex the ego strength of Rosemarie was weak.

Complexes are projected. This was also the case in Rosemarie. She projected the complex as phobic anxiety in situations where she had to take the bus. She saw the bus ride as a constricting situation where she could not escape and therefore reacted with panic. In particular, the bus slowing down caused such feelings. She also projected the complex in situations when her children came home from school. She was waiting in fear that she would not to be able to satisfy her and the children's needs. 'I'll be a puppet, I do everything for the kids, probably I am exaggerating, but I cannot help it', she explained.

The treatment focused on this inner conflict, on the one hand the hippie aspect, on the other the selfless mother aspect. The treatment focused on the loss of self-esteem, her identity and the setting of boundaries in relation to the children, generally her ego strength and improving her perception and differentiation opportunities.

Suddenly she stopped coming to psychotherapy. She had cancelled an appointment because of illness. Since my schedule in practice was relatively full, and I did not schedule the sessions myself, I 'lost sight' of the patient, but also wondered whether her freedom-loving aspect had now affected the psychotherapy.

One day, after two months, she arranged a new appointment. She wanted to talk about her mother. The bus phobia was mastered. She explained that she realized each time on the bus that she fell into her basic feeling. She thinks, 'I'm not locked up here, I can get out'. She was able to calm the panic and put up with it. In other words, she could take back her complex projection in the bus. She was also able to reduce her Xanax use permanently and her sleep problems had improved.

Furthermore, she said she could now better accept that she could not have a fourth child. She was less focused on her children and gave herself more leeway. So far so good. The remaining problem was now her mother, with whom she went on holiday every year with her family.

The following is a fragment of the first hour after two months' break. The client sat first as usual, half turned away, but changed her seating position in the course of the conversation several times. She looked nervous. First, she described the problem with her mother. The whole family had been visiting her over Christmas in the mountains. During this time, she experienced the mother as abusive. Apparently she interrupted the client often and wanted to convince her of other solutions. She ignored counterarguments but responded snappily. Then she served the family a five-course meal, which was boring for the kids because they had to remain seated. Rosemarie complained that she knew this self-sacrificing behaviour of the mother from earlier, but suddenly, from one day to the next, this care can tip over into a snappy, depressed attitude. These changes were difficult to endure.

Interestingly, now the sacrificing attitude of the mother moved to the centre, after Rosemarie had begun to move away from her own victim role. She no longer accepted this behaviour from her mother. 'And how did you react emotionally to her comments?' I asked. 'I got a helpless rage, but I also have sympathy for her. I know she means well. I wanted to help her always; I had so much wanted that she could change'. 'And that is possible?' 'It's not! She is focused on her role which makes me suffer by it and also annoys me. Now I have decided to stop spending all my holidays with my kids with her'.

I asked about her fantasies, and at the same time a picture arose in me. She explained that she saw her mother as something that was small and fragile. I saw in the countertransference a spider that pulled the threads of life; my fantasy was more related to the perpetrator part, the patient more to the victim part of the mother's image. She continued: 'I always fought against this small and fragile thing that I perceived also with my grand-mother, I ran away, and yet it has now caught up with me'. I thought to myself, probably this was the reason for giving birth to several children and the wish to enjoy life intensely with children, education, etc. She was afraid to be as the mother and grandmother and felt it was a 'doomsday' to be silent, bitter and depressed. The atmosphere in the intersubjective space had now changed completely. The sometimes angry sometimes 'cool' woman had suddenly become a frightened but serious woman who realized the black hole that threatened her life energy. She started to describe the nothingness and took advantage of the therapeutic vessel to verbalize these new feelings and thoughts.

C.G. Jung once remarked that if the black queen of depression knocks on the door, then don't send her away, but ask her in and ask what her concern is. Therefore, I asked about these kind of feelings. She replied: 'I suppose I perceive these negative feelings better, I feel myself and my limits generally better, but my easygoing nature has now disappeared in this nothingness'. 'This is sad, I understand', I replied. I could imagine that she had to bury her adolescent part (the hippie part, or the *puella aeternus*). The world had become borders. 'My problem is that while I feel better than half a year ago, I do not clearly see the road ahead of me. I also feel guilty because I leave my mother alone, I cannot help her', she continued sadly.

I interpreted her grief as loss of freedom possibilities. It would have been better to remain empathic, to stay on the intersubjective level of emotional attunement, instead of going on the cognitive level. Because she responded in a confused way, I felt the interpretation overwhelmed her. At this moment, in which the protective barrier of coolness and anger collapsed and uncertainty became obvious, my remark unsettled her. She said: 'Everyone says to me, I would have sooner separated from your mother, who causes of course more guilt'. I succeeded again reacting empathically. Maybe she had 'not heard' my remark, but possibly also led me back by pointing to more empathic remarks of others to bring me back to her. It was noticeable that she looked at me again at the moment of my empathic remark.

Amid the archetypal maelstrom of depression and angry escape into autonomy this patient needed empathy in order to develop better feeling and perception skills. A moment of meeting had been initially made void by my interpretation; however, the patient led me back to again correspond to her feelings.

In retrospect, there are probably times when interpretations are the more useful methods, as well as times when the intersubjective method of affect attunement is more effective.

Paul and the wise old woman

I present below an extract from the work with a client – we'll call him Paul – where one can observe the influence of a positive grandmother and the archetypal experience of a wise old woman.

The 39-year-old patient came into psychotherapy because of congestion symptoms. Paul felt wiped out by his work as a nurse in a hospital. The daily tension left his body stiff; he moved jerkily around the therapy room. He complained of dizziness and lightheadedness, he was not really there. (A dissociation test he filled out yielded high values.) He described also a depressive mood and dissatisfaction in his relationship with his partner. It was clear that he adapted himself both in work as in relationships and that he lost his own feelings. He worked more like a machine. The trigger of the crisis was layoffs of other employees, so he had to take on more work. He also criticized the low esteem of his superiors, which weakened his motivation. The diagnosis was of exhaustion depression, and dissociative tendencies were evident.

In his first interview the patient was emotionally absent, tense and stiff. He looked younger than he actually was, perhaps because he was dressed in a young and fashionable way. He gave much attention to his appearance and went regularly to the hairdresser. He mentioned his homosexuality in the initial consultation. This was the reason why he had moved to a city in Switzerland, because his previous environment was not welcoming for homosexuals.

The history revealed that Paul was 4 years old, his brother had been 6, when his parents separated. According to the client the reason for the separation was his fun-loving young mother, who felt she missed a part of life due to her children. The client described his father as very strict and rigid; duty was paramount. The mother would not have endured this attitude and was too weak to fight back. After the divorce, the children remained with their father. The obsessive father had fought vehemently and relentlessly for them and finally the mother gave in because she wanted to avoid further damage suffered by the troubled and unsettled children. Living with his father was hard and controlled by a precise timetable. After school Paul and his brother had to help with gardening, cooking, distributing letters, etc. The brother was somewhat stronger and escaped where he could. Paul feared his father. He said that as a child he was constantly tense and on alert. His father did not beat him, but he was loud, threatening and there was trouble if something was not done on time. He spent about one weekend per month with the mother; visits were this rare because of the conflict with the father, who did not want the children go often to the mother.

When Paul was 12 years old he finally turned to the youth welfare office. He wanted to move to his mother; in the end, he prevailed after many attempts. He had to grow up quickly, he said dryly in the first interview.

The two sons spent almost every second weekend with the paternal grandmother. Although the father's relationship with his mother was distant, he did not object to these visits.

One day, after a few months of psychotherapy, Paul spoke at some length about this grandmother. The transformation that Paul went through in the conversation was amazing. He remembered that he was allowed to watch his grandmother cooking. She allowed him to decorate salad with parsley; he was allowed to add flour to the cake bowl and swing the dough. Unexpectedly, a number of other descriptive memories appeared, which I could easily follow: he remembered a yellow kitchen with yellow walls, a yellow plastic tablecloth on the kitchen table and brown soil. He remembered the smells of the morning meal. There were always fried potatoes with milk; he sat at dinner on the stove. The picture that he drew was warm, with the kitchen, the food and the grandmother. While he had looked dazed at the beginning of the hour, now there was a crowd of memories of an archetypal grandmotherly experience that came to the surface. While Paul usually spoke rather haltingly, he now spoke with great verbiage, looking at me. Suddenly he felt himself, he said, to have ground under his feet. The atmosphere at this moment was touching, cheerful and relaxed. And for a moment a meeting between him and me was possible, caused by his inner image of the grandmother, which otherwise he rather avoided.

The Jungian Jean Knox speaks of various selves that are stored depending on the experience of the self with others and of internalizing these relationship patterns (Knox, 2012). I suspect that this patient stored by dissociative processes other images with his grandmother, as with other caregivers, such as with the mother and the father.

He never spoke of his father to the grandmother, he was a taboo subject. The client thought she had felt certain that he had not felt comfortable, but said nothing. She knew unconsciously nevertheless the right cure. She showed him the world of smells, the spices, the colours of the food, and so brought the child some relaxation and peace. Surprised, he added that he had not had those memories as an adult, but now he knew why he baked so passionately (e.g. ring cake with vanilla or plum compote with hot vanilla sauce!). In the course of another session the patient compared this experience with a yellow, warm circle, which he kept in his heart. An unconscious experience had become conscious. The memory of the warm, yellow kitchen with the working grandmother served Paul henceforth as a possible resource.

Psychotherapy continued; the grandmother was soon forgotten, too insistent were his everyday problems with sick leave, termination of his job and a dispute with his partner. He wanted clarification in all these areas. Alone he could hardly concentrate and needed therapy as a place that helped him to remain focused. Again and again drowsiness and dizziness seized him. His transference was marked on the one hand by hope that I could help, and on the other hand by feelings of distance and subliminal distrust because of his negative parental images. I kept this transference 'in the pocket' as the Jungian Kathrin Asper once said in a lecture. My countertransference was more influenced by motherliness. He looked like a dishevelled young man (despite his fashionable hairstyle!) who tried tirelessly to make contact with others, but constantly drifted away.

When he found a new job, his condition improved. He also dared in the evenings to go out again. He said the relationship with his partner was marked by boredom and an emphasis on material values. His partner earned much more money than he and bought expensive designer furniture and exclusive suits. He felt trapped in the almost museum-like apartment; he was much more 'alternatively' predisposed and happy in nature. On the other hand, his partner gave him security, and he feared a separation.

His conflict of control and submission occupied us in the coming months. I suspected he suppressed aggressive impulses, especially separation aggression which was unconsciously present, probably as dizziness. His negative father complex implied a dominant, bossy, cold father, whereas he developed feelings of fear and insecurity, the cognitions of worthlessness and inferiority, and a submissive, dissociative or controlling behaviour. His ego strengths were weak. But he began to question the persona of his friend, which I interpreted positively. He was ready to dare more and to be more expansive. He also began to engage in further education.

This was followed by a setback after a few months. He was accustomed to visiting bars, where he met other homosexuals and had different sexual affairs – and fell promptly in love. The man in question was not responsive, which threw the client into a deep hole. His dissociation strategies took over and at such a moment the following meeting took place.

Paul sat opposite me, paralysed and in shock and not by himself. His body seemed stiff and frozen. He lamented the loss – finally he had once again fallen in love, but the other did not want anything to do with him; one night was enough. Paul did not cry, his grief was not notice-able, and my empathy did not reach him. So I asked what kind of image emerges in this situation. An image is sometimes easier to access than an emotion.

He pondered and said he saw himself as a small, thin figure standing in a desert of ice; he was frozen there. I decided to use the method of guided imagery ('Katathym-imaginative Psychotherapie' or KIP). An active imagination by C.G. Jung would have been an excessive demand for this client; it requires more ego strengths.

After the usual relaxation exercise, I asked:

'On the ice desert can you see an end?'
'No, it's all white.'
'Can you try to see from above?'
'Yes. I look down, but it still looks all white.'
'Can you go up even further?'
'Now I can see an end. There, a forest begins.'

The client estimated that the frozen wasteland was about the size of a football field; it was now no longer ice, but covered with snow. I asked him if he wanted to go on. He said yes, but it is very difficult to concen-trate. I put forth some words of comfort. To use many words is more of a hindrance in imagery meeting for the process. I then asked:

'Try to go into your body – what do you see?'
'Only white.'
'Can you try to look at your feet?'
'This is difficult. I see heavy shoes with thick soles. It's unpleasant, to put myself in me. I feel my feet barely. If I succeed, I cram in me, I have a feeling I'm going to be too heavy for the ice, and the ice breaks.'

These sentences offered numerous opportunities for further interventions. However, I opted for the following: 'I think, the ice is wearing you'.

That was a conscious intervention on my part to give security. Such interventions are delivered in KIP only carefully and at the appropriate moment. The patient had previously been the one to give help to others, to take over the responsibility (moods of the father, the ice, the therapist), fears not being kept was therefore normal. He rather controlled his surroundings instead of engaging himself.

The patient remained silent for a moment.

I asked after a while (because protection mechanisms as dissociation should sometimes be taken in order to progress):

'If you follow now the urge to leave, what's happening?'

'This is such a relief'. He took a deep breath and looked relieved. I had to breathe deeply, too, and noticed only now how exhausting the imagination was for both of us. He recovered, and I encouraged him to refocus on his feet. This time he succeeded better and he felt the desire to go to the edge of the forest. His fear was gone, but now he was frozen. Again he reached for his protection and defence mechanism to control the situation. I asked:

'Who could help you there?'
'My grandmother.' He expressed these thoughts spontaneously and surprisingly for both of us.
'Do you see her?'
'Yes. She comes, she says I should not be afraid, I could come with her. I hesitate. As she lifts me onto her back and carries me away.'

The client had insisted on controlling the situation, but the inner unconscious image of the grandmother was stronger and overcame his conscious attitude. I further asked for sensory perceptions in order to improve his body image.

'How is it on the back of grandmother?'
'It's warm.'
'What is happening now?'
'She takes me to the woods. I can feel the soil, the heat of the air. I now feel my feet better.' (He started to cry.)

Later, he told me the grandmother had looked like a very old woman and was quite plump. I assumed, because his own body was very thin, his unconscious includes nourishing aspects, alongside denied and repressed emotions; therefore the chubby old woman emerged from his unconscious. The imagination enhanced his perceptions of feelings.

The psychotherapy is not yet finished, but at least he was able to use the archetypal symbol of the old wise woman from then on in a fruitful way. The inner image of the old wise woman, nourished by his grand-mother experiences, accompanied him from then on and helped him to find safety, and to better endure unbearable feelings and to deal more effectively with his resistances.

Hans and the negative spirit of his grandfather

In recent years, the approach of the intergenerational transmission of trauma has developed. The hypothesis is that there are problems in the children's generation that may arise from severe unconscious conflicts of parents and grandparents. In addition, different generations in families may show up repeating conflicts – as repetition compulsion – of which they are not necessarily aware. This is done by multiple interfamilial transmission processes, argue the psychoanalysts Almuth Massing, Günther Reich and Eckhard Sperling, who dealt particularly with this topic (Massing, Reich & Sperling, 2006; see also Bergmann, Jucovy & Kestenberg, 1995; Laub, 1998). Traumas, resulting from serious ill-nesses, high numbers of deaths, migration problems, war experiences, violence, sexual abuse or strong loyalty conflicts, were the causes of such processes.

Especially wars like the First or Second World War, the 'Third Reich' or the Stalin era left their mark on the affected generations. Role assign-ments and delegations from unresolved conflicts and traumatic experi-ences are passed on from the grandparents to the parents, if they have not worked and emotionally integrated, and are finally unconsciously passed on to the children. The creation of family secrets and myths belong into these defence processes. Personality traits of grandparents and aspects of the parent–grandparent relationship such as frozen grief or shame can emerge in the parent–child relationship (Reich, Massing & Cierpka, 2007). Of course it is possible that new structures and relationship pat-terns between generations can develop, as we shall see in the next chapter.

In recent years in analytical psychology the transgenerational trans-mission of trauma has been intensely debated (Cavalli, 2012; Connolly, 2011; Pickering, 2012). These Jungians emphasize the awareness of sym-bolic forms, so that the patient can give those things a form which he unconsciously carries in himself and has not to do with him. In this work, according to the London Jungian Alessandra Cavalli, the analyst must resist identification with the patient if he wants to help him integrate the traumatic experience in a symbolic form (Cavalli, 2012).

The voiceless ancestors influence the lives of grandchildren, even if they do not know the ancestors and have never experienced something of their suffering. The unconscious of these ancestors influence the unconscious of children, notably if they have not learnt to put their experiences into words or in images. If this is not possible, this experience flies into the unconscious of children and grandchildren, even into the analytic setting until one perceives it, renames, symbolizes and assigns it a place. The Australian Jungian Judith Pickering summarizes this process as follows:

> As analyst we share in bearing unbearable burden of pain that our patients unwittingly inherit. Through the transformational containment of the analytic relationship both analyst and patient may begin to think the unthinkable, dream it into conscious awareness and find language to describe what was once indescribable.
>
> (Pickering, 2012, p. 577)

The analytical space may constitute such intersubjective place where such past emotions can be reflected and symbolized, and the scattered pieces can begin to form a whole.

In this context, Angela Connolly postulates three fundamental aspects of the transgenerational transmission of trauma: the death of time, the death of the language and the death of the narrative (Connolly, 2011). A descendant who is affected by such past trauma can cope only if he agrees that the time has passed, that options are no longer available, if he finds a language for the inner material and if he finds a narrative that puts the inner foreign material in a different time horizon. The foreign material is finally no longer his own, and he learns to separate and thus to develop his own self and identity. A traumatic event has the ability to destroy the internal organization of the first generation, the second grows under this influence and forms a kind of relationship with it. In the third generation, it is assimilated into the self (Connolly, 2011).

The example of a 59-year-old client, Hans, is described in the following. The hypothesis is that mainly the maternal grandfather shaped his unconscious – to the extent that could be seized by the anamnesis. This grandfather had died before the birth of Hans. (I focus below on the connection between grandfather and grandchild and leave aside other important areas, such as the parent or sibling relationships, or the image of women, as this is beyond the scope.)

The family doctor had referred the client to me, as many of his psycho-somatic complaints pointed to psychological roots. He said he was suffering from phantom smells, anxiety, tremor of the eyeballs, fatigue, pain in many parts of his body and tension. Medical investigations revealed arthritis in the feet, otherwise nothing relevant could be found. Asked about the cause of his complaints, he answered: the parlous state in which he grew up. Hans added psychosocial stress situations as he had to change apartment in two years, but was undecided whether he wanted to live in the city, on the land or in the mountains. He added an unsatisfactory relationship with a girlfriend that was staying in a psychiatric hospital at that time. He complained in particular of the non-ecstatic quality of their relationship. In a few years he would retire, but he wished to take early retirement because he felt exhausted and wanted to be able to live. The problem was the finances and his fear of falling out of a structure. The post-retirement design was unclear to him, the future scared him. He suffered from nightmares and a feeling of congestion.

Opposite me sat a rather attractive but somewhat defunct man. (A colleague saw him once in the practice's corridor and mentioned: 'Aha a handsome man!'.) He spoke in monologues for long periods and added problem area to problem area. Now and then he looked at me, but he did not do well with eye contact.

At the first meeting I hardly managed to say something about the accumulation of his problems; I felt overwhelmed and fascinated, but mostly confused. Defensively I was trying to find solid ground and therefore asked for facts. Nevertheless, while listening a first image appeared, namely Walter Benjamin's writing about Paul Klee's 'The Angel of History', which is a picture that represents an angel that is backward-looking, not able to rotate to the future. In 1940 Walter Benjamin wrote about this picture:

> There is a painting by Klee called *Angelus Novus*. It shows an angel who seems about to move away from something he stares. His eyes are wide, his mouth is open, and his wings are spread. This is how the angel of history must look. His face is turned towards the past. Where a chain of events appears before *us*, *he* sees one single catastrophe which keeps piling wreckage upon wreckage and hurls it at his feet. The angel would like to stay, awaken the dead, and make whole what has been smashed. But a storm is blowing from Paradise and has got caught in his wings; it is so strong that the angel can no longer close them. This storm drives him irresistibly into the future

to which his back is turned, while the pile of debris before him grows towards sky. What we call progress, is this *storm*.

(Benjamin, 1940, p. 392)

I supposed a common unconscious occurred. It could not be assessed whether it was by the process of projective identification or an own complex seeing myself as the helpless angel.

As a treatment goal, he stated that he needed help with his future design, he had a panic about the future (*sic*!). He wanted to be able to sleep again, he had to take Temesta every night (a benzodiazepine). He also needed help with his desire to build an ecstatic relationship with a woman. He currently lived in an abysmal situation and in endless futility – he wanted to finally live.

As resources he mentioned art, architecture, literature and erotic themes; these topics gave him something like a meaning. The client was capable of introspection, was intelligent and had a broad cultural knowledge. Some internal working models were stable, such as the handling of his professional situation, which he learned from his now deceased father.

We agreed weekly appointments that he kept from then on. The treatment goal was clarifying his professional and relational future, assistance in orientation and in his own life plan. He supported my suggestion in this regard, to obtain concrete homework. Suspected diagnosis was a post-traumatic stress disorder with psychosomatic symptoms. Noticed also were vague fears, a depressed and an idealistic processing mode, an identity diffusion and dissociative tendencies. From a Jungian perspective, a more or less stable persona could be ascertained that held a strong, unformed inner world. The ego strength was weak and could be flooded at any time with archetypal material.

The biography revealed that his father had been a teacher in a technical artist school. He had led an unremarkable life. The father of the mother was born in Germany and had participated in the First World War as a soldier, including in the Russian campaign. Afterwards he immigrated to Switzerland, where he married and had four children. The youngest, his mother, later had three children, of which the client was the youngest. The older sister graduated from vocational training and practised her profession more or less constantly but for interruptions due to severe depression and several stays in psychiatric hospitals. The brother had recently died – Hans did not know how, and didn't want to know. The brother had learned no profession and fell into drug and alcohol addiction and lived until his death in a dilapidated state. Hans knew that he was often involved with the police. Their relationship was marked by distance. Now, his death had brought to mind the full extent of his dysfunctional family.

The patient could hardly remember his childhood. He knew from stories that he had been weaned after three weeks due to a chest infection of his mother. He also witnessed the eyes of the mother as avoidant, and there were no memories of her providing security or safety. 'I felt managed from my mother', he said. It seems as if he had been pushed by her into a disorganized space.

Cavalli argues in another context that children of traumatized parents have a disorganized attachment to these. The trauma of the parent's functions as a disorganizing force means the attachment becomes unpredictable for the child and impairs the ability for security and empathy. When the traumatized person is the mother, this process is much more dramatic than with the father, because the child is confronted in the womb directly with traumatized material (Cavalli, 2012).

If the mother is traumatized, her experiences can freely flow into the child, so he is overwhelmed. The child experiences her unconscious fears, impulses and other oppressed or unintegrated parts as 'negative attributions' in himself, which become an integral part of the child (Lieberman, 1999, p. 737). Cavalli refers to Fraiberg (1980), Faimberg (2005) and Perelberg (1997), and states:

> Where there is no representation, there can be no separation, only identification. If the maternal unconscious is inhabited by ghosts and void (her own or her husband's), she will not be able to transmit to her infant an internal sense of security and a version of herself as a mother who can protect her child from her own, her husband's and her child's destructive phantasy.
>
> (Cavalli, 2012, p. 610)

Although the patient spoke about his mother a few times, I did not manage to develop a mental image of her. She remained strangely faceless and colourless. I suspected the client gave me this impression unconsciously. As Cavalli writes, he had probably no internal stable image of the mother which could give him security. Even on her deathbed she had shifted away from him when he tried to take her hand. At least, this was his interpretation of the twitch of her hand.

His mother died shortly after he started the treatment. Her funeral urn and that of the deceased brother from a few months earlier remained at a preliminary site as neither Hans nor his sister could bury both at a final location. This family lived in an intermediate realm, I thought, in which there was no time in the sense of past, present and future, as Angela Connolly describes. In limbo everything is equally present and magically populated by spirits of the dead, of threatening feelings as extreme helplessness and futility. Hans called it the stowage of life, where life can't take place. In the countertransference I realized slight aggressiveness with such statements and experienced a feeling of constriction.

The stowage appeared in numerous dreams and nightmares. An example from the early days of analysis follows. He described in a monotone manner a frequently recurring dream: 'The night sky is full of streaks, contrails, crisscross, very threatening, I'm lying in a bassinet'. Initially it was not clear if he had this dream previously or now. This dream remained just a picture; I couldn't discuss it with him. The vision was as foreign material, standing in the room without an emotion such as panic, although he mentioned the threat of the image. I noticed the association of a sky full of planes and bombs, but at that time I had not yet understood this association.

The patient mostly continued to speak of more dreams or situations that he remembered; for example, in one dream he was trapped in a kind of engine of a tractor – he could not move and if someone had started the tractor he would have been crushed. The feeling was claustrophobic, but he did not feel it, he only spoke about it. Or he was in a railway carriage, jammed in an extremely enclosed situation, like a mummy in a sarcophagus. He rattled off these stories; it was not possible for me to embrace them. He added at the same time that in the evening he watched technical videos of the *Apollo* mission on YouTube, where the astronauts were trapped in a capsule and flown into space, their lives hanging from a thread.

We could better speak about these videos. Finally, the term of the womb emerged in the analytic space. He reacted surprised, but again the term did not stick, no associations could be developed. But he added: 'There is a kind of a secret in my family. At me something very big has grown, that is effective in the background and applies a patina on my feelings'. This was a phrase that stood out like a lump in the room and could not be more verbalized. Another piece of debris had been thrown into the analytical vessel.

By and by, he nevertheless began to enrich his dreams with feelings and historical associations, and started the work of anchoring a narrative in time. His mother, in the sense of the French psychoanalyst André

Green, had been a 'dead mother' (Green, 2011) who was not emotionally available and couldn't meet the emotional needs of the children. His mother was possibly herself traumatized. But what had traumatized his mother?

We must remember, his grandfather had been a German soldier in the First World War, including on the Eastern Front in the Russian campaign. The client did not know much about him except that this grandfather had to blow up houses, churches and buildings, and that the war was terrible for him. He was very religious and had trouble following the order to blow up churches. From a church he had removed an image from a frame with his bayonet and taken it home; it showed 'Jesus in the Garden of Olives'. Only after this did he blow up the church. (This picture is owned by the client now.) Jesus was anxious in the Garden of Olives, about the crucifixion, and asked his father to let pass the cup to him. I thought to myself, this grandfather had probably had similar feelings of fear and disgust like Jesus and therefore took the effort upon himself to save the image and to bring it, in midst of war, home. In countertransference fantasies I began to enrich his stories with considerations that could anchor his story in time, so that a narrative could arise.

The client had also begun to take away the focus from his complaints and problems and paid more attention to his ancestors. He wondered why he felt attracted to old war documentary films on YouTube, where people screamed and fled from burning houses, or films of submarines or a song from the Second World War with the line 'Enjoy the war, the peace will be terrible'. The films calmed him, so he could fall asleep afterwards. The client had unconsciously begun to seek his own narrative for his archetypal images and to escape the magical effect of the grandfather. It seems that he was looking for his inner images in external correspondence, headed by the implicit knowledge that works associatively, but has no reflexive function, logic or hierarchy (Graf & Schacter, 1985). He did not know why he was looking for these videos on YouTube; they had not (yet) formed a symbolic function and remained fragmentary, but he had started the search.

We started to think about it together, how the Russian campaign was for his grandfather, how it was to bomb a church, how his unknown grandfather was and what experience his mother had in pregnancy. The client had previously related everything to himself, but now the focus changed; he was able to empathize with others better. Before, he was overwhelmed with all the material. We thought dreamily (rêverie) about grandfather and mother. At least this rêverie allowed him to maintain belief in the good, with the hope that structure eventually would prevail over chaos.

He brought another dream in a further session, in which he was trapped in a musty crypt. Around him he suspected deaths. He wanted to extricate himself and sought a halt, and suddenly he caught a hand. This hand was dead. He freed himself, and made with his other hand a revolutionist's fist, I will manage to win! He then saw an opening in the crypt where a woman with an oval open shirt stood. (His associations: a *mandorla* (gloriole), a vagina, a shroud with a black hole.) He said cheekily: 'Now we're going to fuck [have sex]!'

Without going into detail, I wanted to point out that the archetypal themes of birth, sexuality, woman, of death and life appeared side by side and replaced the terrifying nightmares of death. Also, the client acted more autonomously in this dream.

The more strongly he situated the images of war in the previous generation and was able to speak about shame, the better he managed to get involved with his unconscious material, with his archetypal images. Fear, shame and guilt paralysed him so far and contributed to his defences, which blocked his development. The feelings of futility became weaker, and he learned to better differentiate what were his feelings and what had been his mother's and his grandfather's feelings.

He stopped watching war movies. He ended his relationship, began discontinuing the various drugs slowly and ended his 'doctor shopping'. Six months later he took the treatment of his inflammation into his own hands and began to switch to a vegan diet. His diverse inflammations declined, he claimed. He tried to eat organic food, which could also be understood symbolically. He decided unconsciously to only incorporate the good. His self-efficacy strengthened, his ability to act began to grow and he started to clean up. The concept of homework has been retained to emphasize the present and the here and now.

He got to know a new woman with whom he had happy moments. Now in many areas of his life he made decisions, even if the ideal of a Dionysian attitude to life was still his guiding principle. His preferred idealistic defence strategy had been to seek a Dionysian life in fusion with a woman instead of experiencing threatening, empty or meaningless images.

The following case vignette is described in which he told another dream. As always, he greeted me respectfully and then sat down in the armchair. By this time the monologue had largely stopped; he looked directly at me. He told the following dream:

I hear someone down at the entrance call me up: 'Do not let it enter', said someone. Nevertheless, I open the door, because someone is outside. There is a cat in front, a very beautiful, black, 80 kg heavy beast, muscled, with a smooth beautiful skin that shines like an emerald. It's a panther, it looks elegant and nimble. I repel him with an old 40 cm long scale, carved into millimetres, and can prevent the animal from coming into my apartment. One person may accompany the cat.

The atmosphere in the room was now intense and crackling; he was touched – I felt in the countertransference a strong sense of vitality. The panther image stimulated the mood and created a numinous quality through the archetypal image of the wild cat. One can also speak of a now moment. In the unconscious of the patient an archetypal image had developed, which he shared with me and of which I was also touched, so strong that I was at its mercy for moments and lost the therapeutic attitude. The feeling was reinforced by the fact that he associated on the one hand his girlfriend, but also me, with the image of the panther.

It is possible that he pushed that feeling by a mechanism of projective identification in me. I felt diffuse, that a man–woman issue was addressed that both gave up the role of the analytic pair for a moment; I realized pleasure and *joie de vivre*. He pointed naughtily to me saying that I also only wore black dresses today. His transference irritated me until I could adopt an analytical attitude again and talk to him about the dream.

He associated the scale with one from high school. Previously, he had gathered such and compared them with regard to their length with each other. Further, he associated the cat with a wild, impulsive, unpredictable, dangerous and powerful animal. The big cat was associated with power, sexuality, vitality and energy.

Next was discussed to what extent the vital panther had to do with his masculinity and less with women. He held out his scale of puberty to the image of masculinity, with which he wanted to keep the panther at bay. I wondered if the scale symbolized a superego aspect at the level of a teenager who was just enough in the face of the danger of his id-wishes to send the panther away.

Another interpretation offers a more positive view. The panther and thus vitality knocked symbolically on the door, as a positive archetypal symbol which replaced the death images of capsules, machines, wombs and caves. He could only hold out towards the danger of the symbolic wooden scale (penis symbol?). Nevertheless, the life energy had penetrated the analytic space and we both felt it for a moment. The patient took the hint, not simply to delegate the vital energy to women.

Three weeks later he brought another crypt-dream in which the hand, which he took, was only half dead. His thought was immediate: oh, now I must spring into action! He turned towards the opening of the tomb, where this time no woman stood. He needed to creep alone to the opening, he said almost with regret in his voice. He had to abandon his delegation his unconscious told him.

The analysis is not yet finished, but his ability to develop a symbolic attitude and his self-efficacy skills have grown. He began to take his life in hand. There was much sadness, shame and guilt regarding the earlier events of his grandfather and mother, but the experience of these feelings allowed him to live more in the present and to let go of the magic of the past.

Sabine and Mother Holle-grandmother

In the literature, much has been written about the transgenerational transmission of trauma in recent years (for example, see Rauwald, 2013). This research is very important for on the unconscious influences on parents and grandchildren. There are also cases where grandparents do not pass their trauma on to the parents, or cases where, although they pass them on to the parents, they don't pass them on to the grandchildren; their impact on the grandchildren is positive. The unconscious transmission follows winding paths and general predictions are impossible.

Even in psychoanalytic debate, reference is made to these winding paths. The reference to the 'ghosts in the nursery' of psychoanalysts Fraiberg *et al.* (1975) evoked a great response and a number of other studies have been published on this subject (e.g. Barrows, 2004; Duggin, 2008). The concept of Fraiberg and her colleagues was not without objections. The metaphor 'angels in the nursery' was proposed by psychoanalytic child psychologists. Parents who could make, as children, positive experiences with their parents and who felt understood and accepted could give those feelings to their own children and strengthen their feeling of security, even if they were also traumatized by the same parents. These child psychologists argue that not all parents pass on their 'spirits' and not all grandparents traumatize the next generation, even if they were themselves traumatized (Lieberman, Padro'n, Van Horn & Harries 2005). Alicia Lieberman and her colleagues do not deny the 'ghosts', but they see 'ghosts' and 'angels' in the nursery in a dynamic tension side by side. They received strong agreement from Zuckerman and Zuckerman (2005) but also criticism from others (e.g. Drell, 2005).

The case of a grandmother is outlined below, who was herself traumatized, but did not pass on the trauma. She represented an 'angel', even a 'Mother Holle' to the grandchild.

The 41-year-old female patient made an appointment because she was suffering from panic attacks and felt helpless. Opposite me sat a small, slim, alert-looking woman. She had a sympathetic aura and aroused immediate positive feelings in me. She was lively, gesturing to make me understand what she suffered.

She grew up as the middle child of three children in Germany. The parents immigrated from the GDR to Germany and had strict educational principles. The patient, let's call her Sabine, described in particular the father as a rigid, authoritarian man who could not bear to be contradicted. The mother also had to bow to this. From puberty she suffered from severe panic attacks that continue to this day. The patient suspected a connection with her father's education.

In the initial interview and subsequent meetings she talked about various negative experiences in childhood, always looking at me trustingly. Every time this occured, I had an impulse to want to protect her. I wondered why she could constellate this emotion in me. It was only later in the therapy I understood.

The panic attacks could occur almost anywhere, but especially in tunnels. She had to go every day by train through a tunnel, which was not very long – about three minutes – but she had trouble and panicked every time. When the train stopped in the tunnel, which had happened, she felt particularly bad. Further, she feared the authority of her supervisor, who sometimes reacted angrily towards her; in contrast, other employees knew how to deal with him, whereas she would think about his remarks for days. When asked about her relationship, she created a positive image of her husband: 'He supports me very much and I feel lifted by him. I have known him since the age of 19, he helped me to move out of my parents' flat'. Their daughter was 12 years old and developed normally. The client therefore had different internal working models. She managed to enter positive, trusting relationships, but also relationships marked by fears.

In the course of the psychotherapy, background information about her panic attacks emerged and it turned out that she was suffering not only from panic attacks, but also generalized anxiety and various phobias; she was more seriously ill than I thought at first. She avoided travelling by plane. If possible she would live only in a narrow radius around her city. Spending holidays in another country was difficult for her. She quickly lost her sense of security when she moved too far away from home. Many things concerned and scared her; she was afraid of people in general. In addition, a bad-tempered neighbour or the wishes of her mother could trigger violent feelings of guilt.

At that point in the psychotherapy I suspected a complex post-traumatic stress disorder; I asked myself again why she was so trusting of me, having general fears and a rather high distrust level.

As to the causes of her fears she mentioned that she was sent by her parents every summer for several weeks to the south of Germany 'for regeneration'. Her parents justified this procedure with the local fresh air and good food. So when she was between three and 14 years old, she was shipped there every summer, though she did not want to go, and struggled and felt homesick. Sometimes she was accompanied by her siblings, sometimes not, if they had been accommodated elsewhere. When she returned home, she sometimes no longer knew her parents, they had become strange.

'Later I found out that my parents wanted to go on holiday somewhere abroad for the sake of their quiet', she said, looking at me helplessly. 'They wanted to be left alone', she repeated, soberly. She was silent. I was surprised. How would you describe parents who send their children away for several weeks with strangers? I did not understand. I tried to empathize but was only partially successful. Objectively speaking, the attitude of the parents was shocking; but saying this, expressing my indignation strongly, the patient could become locked and would defend the parents. So I replied only: 'That must not be easy for you and may be incomprehensible'. She nodded, yes, she did not understand and she still didn't understand it today. Then she added, moreover, that because of an illness she had to go to a clinic several times. There, too, she suffered from severe homesickness and got into such a rage that nurses sometimes had to tie her down. Her parents did not understand her rage. The picture, as she was handcuffed to the hospital bed, dipped into the present time as a fixed image again and again.

The image of the hospital situation, the sending away during the summer holidays and the authoritarian father were in the background of her current symptoms. As a child she suffered probably from overflowing archetypal fears without having enough parental support and security. She responded with inner excitement and fury, which her situation only made worse by the lack of understanding from others. In the analysis, therefore, first her feelings of safety had to be strengthened and then she needed to get acquainted with grief, rage and pain and learn to endure them. At the beginning, gestures, facial expressions and content of the discussions were congruent, but only partially connected to the emotions. The patient was not sad; she spoke only about sad contents. Her fears covered these feelings.

The time was not yet right for this procedure. Looking for inner resources we found the maternal grandmother. (To save space, other important influences such as the mother or siblings are neglected here.) She very well remembered her since she often stayed with her. This grandmother was very kind and dear to her. She had white hair and red cheeks, 'as Mother Holle' the patient said with a smile and slightly hopping in her chair. The patient referred to the fairy tale and thus to stored memories in the personal unconscious as well as to stories about archetypal images of Mother Holle in the collective unconscious. Intermingling a personal and a collective level, the experiencing of the grand-motherly figure gained more depth. Yet another reason for mentioning Mother Holle was central. The patient fairy tale unconsciously increased the intersubjective space, as we both were able to get an idea of Mother Holle, whereas I did not have a picture of her grandmother in mind.

If we work on the premise that a patient unconsciously projects different roles onto the therapist, one might argue that my patient offered me the role of Mother Holle, perhaps in the desire for a motherly nurturing figure, but perhaps also to spare the therapist her painful material. Furthermore, my experiences with my own grandmother were activated. With one I experienced positive experiences, the other I barely knew, so I probably unconsciously accepted the role assigned. These unconscious processes in the intersubjective space between both can probably never dissolve completely. Also, the assigned roles can even change during a session, depending on the expectations, fantasies and contents of the talks between the two parties.

In the patient's memory the grandmother wore a chequered apron and shoved a roast in the oven. She always invited many guests. Shortly before her death she said to the patient: 'Oh Bee, you'll have forgotten me very quickly when I am dead'. The patient came to tears as she told it, and I was instantly touched in the present moment. The patient continued, 'I am thinking of her every day, I talk with her. I ask her what I should do, and she answers me.' Sabine's words came fast. She had a lot of memories stored, which filled in a way the void left by her parents. The words spilled out and influenced the intersubjective space. It seemed that this grandmother was the reason for the positive transference, and which enabled her to get involved in the therapy at all. Of course, it could also be that she thus avoided negative feelings.

The grandmother's hair looked like cotton candy and Sabine would always get candy from her; her parents would not allow it, but the grandmother said: 'Nonsense, you must eat this'. I asked what the grandmother had said to the annual sending away. She said that she didn't know about it and if so, then she would probably have supported her mother. Also, there was enough to eat in the south of Germany (the subject of food seemed to be very important in this family). The image of the grandmother got a crack, but this was not noticed by the patient. She retained the ideal Mother Holle image, the archetype image of an old wise woman. The complex, which she developed with respect to these experiences, differed greatly from the parent complexes. On the one hand, there was a positive grandmother complex, on the other hand, negative parent complexes. Jean Knox speaks of different selves, of different experiences with others and various internalized relationship patterns that are developed during childhood (Knox, 2012).

But why did she experience the grandmother so positive? This grandmother had experienced two World Wars, raised six children in a bombed-out German city and knew what hunger, poverty and violence were. Sabine's mother described her as a terrible and constantly complaining mother, who had little empathy with the children. But as she got older, she changed. Sabine said her grandmother declared, when 80 years old, that the last ten years had been the best in her life! The patient never heard complaints; she was charming and enjoyed life to the fullest. An example: the two flew together to the United States (before the flight phobia began), travelled around, rode a roller coaster (!) and visited many cities. In her hometown, the grandmother struck out on her own and did not act like an old woman.

> She drank champagne and 'Berliner Weisse mit Schuss' [light wheat beer with syrup]. I was allowed to drink a sip when I was a little older. We also went to movies. Oh, she was such a thoroughly positive woman. I send every day prayers to her, she was like Mother Holle or as an angel with a magic wand and stars in her hair

Sabine said enthusiastically.

Grandmother and granddaughter shared a common wavelength and common interests; the patient unconsciously benefited as a child from the archetypal image of the grandmother, the archetypal image of the nourishing, sheltering grandmother with her *joie de vivre*, the kindness and love for this frightened child. This child may in turn have aroused precisely these characteristics within the grandmother, by her curiosity, interest and openness to new ideas.

Panic and instability in the present were of course also available, but this patient was able to go into another world – like the girl in the story of Mother Holle – recover and develop in the archetypal world of Mother Holle, far from her world of origin. The grandmother saturated partially Sabine's attachment needs, thus positive internal working models and complexes could be developed, e.g. with her husband or could trigger positive feelings in others.

In the later analysis the inner image of the grandmother became an internal figure that helped her to face her frightening inner demons, which provoked panic attacks and vague fears, and helped her when she started to connect the different relationship experiences with each other, and to face the fear and fight against the demanding neighbour or the capricious boss. Integrating and working through negative experiences and feelings is the goal of any analysis. However, the mobilization of positive complexes in the sense of activation of resources is also central to any psychotherapy. Interestingly, the grandmother was the resource, a grandmother who was herself traumatized but heavily modified, perhaps, in exchange with her grandchild. Because with Sabine she could again be young and try things she might not have tried otherwise.

This potential for change one must probably concede to grandparents in principle. Bertolt Brecht wrote in 1939 a little story 'Die unwürdige Greisin' ('The undignified crone') (Brecht, 1939). He described a 72-year-old woman who changed after her husband had died. Although he had a literary-related distance to the text, one can read his sympathy for the old woman between the lines. Adapted to her life and discreetly mastered in the everyday with the four children, and with quite meagre resources, her behaviour changed dramatically after her husband's death. She didn't take one of her children into her large, old house as they wanted, and she didn't inform them of what she was doing in her life. One of her children, a book printer who remained in the town, took over writing to the other children from time to time, some of whom lived abroad. Outraged and shocked he wrote that she went to the movies, often in miserable, poorly ventilated premises, old bowling alleys, where murders and tragedies of passion were displayed; places where usually only teenagers went or, because of darkness, loving couples.

When the children gossiped that she wasted money, the old woman did not respond. She also broke up with her old coffee acquaintances. Her interest in children and grandchildren was limited, but she began to take an interest in young people, encouraged a young girl and began to travel. In short, she allowed herself in old age finally to live after she had previously led an unremarkable existence in which she had adapted to the wishes of others. Her children grumbled, but this did not bother her. She went to the cobbler, a Social Democrat, took the kitchen maid to the local assemblies where loud, funny people were, where she also played cards and drank a glass of red wine. She seemed to lead a fairly active and fine life, but which no longer met with the value systems of her children. Brecht himself seems to have secretly had great respect for this old woman. His conclusion was: she had a tiny little face with many wrinkles and a thin-lipped but wide mouth. Very small, but not petty. She had savoured the long years of slavery and the brief years of freedom and consumed the bread of life to the last seed.

C.G. Jung and the positive spirit of his grandfather

This chapter describes the positive effects of a deceased grandparent on the individuation of a grandchild. If there is no real relationship between grandparent and grandchild, the possibility of an archetypal influence is greater, especially if the grandparent represents a strong role model or an ideal image, family myths include him and the parents are seen as weak compared to him. The result of such a positive grandfather complex for grandchildren consists in an inner orientation with ideal expectation patterns, to become like his grandfather.

A good example of such an archetypal effect of a paternal grandfather is C.G. Jung's grandfather, who had the same name – namely C.G. Jung – and with whom Jung dealt mainly during puberty and adolescence. Jung did not know his grandparent in person; he lived 1794–1864 and was by far the most famous and most respected ancestor in Basle society (Bair, 2003, p. 58).

C.G. Jung's grandfather had studied science and medicine in Heidelberg and then moved to Berlin. He was also interested in literature, so soon after arriving he entered the literary circle around the Schlegel brothers, Ludwig Tieck and Friedrich Schleiermacher. His rebellious spirit criticized the Catholic Church; he turned in this matter to the famous theologian Friedrich Schleiermacher. He wrote about him: 'Karl Gustav Jung has informed me of his intention to convert from the Roman

Catholic Church, in which he was born and brought up and confront the Protestant Church' (E. Jung, 1910, p. 6, cited in A. Jung, 2011, p. 661) He soon after left the Catholic Church. He also became involved in the political circles of the Fraternities and gymnastic clubs, was mistakenly taken into custody and spent 13 months in prison. Later, he was released without trial, but was expelled from Prussia.

He moved to Switzerland and due to fortunate circumstances soon became professor of medicine at the University of Basel – he had been taken into the university on a recommendation by the famous German scientist Alexander von Humboldt. As a professor of medicine, he engaged in manifold areas; he was soon regarded as a well-known scientist, avid Freemason and advocate of democratic ideals. The Freemasons chose him for eight years as a Master of the Basel Masonic lodge. Finally, he even became Grand Master of the Grand Lodge Alpina Swiss (Dieterich, 2001 p. 186). He also restructured and renewed the medical institution and set up a new institution for the accommodation and education of mentally ill children ('Anstalt der Hoffnung' – 'Institute for hope'). He also claimed courageously to build a psychiatric institution (Jacobi, 1973, p. 403) and published some articles in this respect in which he called for an institution at which patients try to heal psychologically instead of putting them in a detention centre (Bair, 2003, p. 23).

In the politically and militarily troubled times of the early nineteenth century, his salary as a professor was not secure, and was suddenly cut in half. He could come to terms with it, as he noted in his diary (A. Jung, 2011, p. 661). Security seemed less important to him, as suggested by his three marriages also. However, towards fellow human beings he was a strict patriarch with an irascible temperament (Bair, 2003, p. 23). All biographers described Jung's grandfather as a patriarchal figure with a strong social, liberal and democratic commitment, as an enlightened free thinker and scientist.

Thus, it is conceivable that he became an archetypal image to Jung on which he could project the image of strength for his orientation, particularly as the relationship with his parents was marked by inconsistency, confusion, anxiety and negative emotions. The paternal grandfather, however, appeared to be an ideal role model. Children cannot help but identify with the values, rules and ideals that evolve in a family, since they convey a sense of belonging and security. Kids identify in the early stages of development with initially idealized parent and grandparent figures, with their supposed or real strengths that protect and guide. This is the opinion of family therapists and psychoanalysts such as Günter Reich, Almuth Massing and Manfred Cierpka (Reich *et al.*, 2007, p. 18). But why were the parents not the appropriate role models?

Jung described impressively in *Memories, Dreams, Reflections* (Jung, 1989) the atmosphere of his childhood and feelings about his parents. He noted that his childhood was marked by painful abandonment by his ailing mother, who repeatedly, sometimes for months, went to hospital and sometimes also separated from his father. Jung often had nightmares of her; she seemed uncanny, as a seer, both as a strange animal or a priestess in a bear's cave (Jung, 1989, p. 50). He tried to deal with these fears in a game. He recalled: 'My first concrete memory of games dates from my seventh or eighth year. I was passionately fond of playing with bricks, and built towers which I then rapturously destroyed by an "earthquake"' (Jung, 1989, p. 18). The 'earthquake' probably symbolized the insecure attachment to his mother. The two personalities of his mother – one sweet and nice, another eerie and mysterious – frightened the little Jung; he had nightmares of things that were once large, once small. Starting at seven he suffered from pseudo croup, with choking attacks that can be understood as a psychosomatic reaction.

His easily irritated father, pastor by profession, with doubts about God, could not really be a role model for Jung. He perceived him as weak. There were also tensions in the marriage; his father was disappointed by his mother, which was perhaps one of the reasons he was chronically depressed, irritable and bad tempered. The thus created family feeling seemed not to have been very stable. It is possible that his image of the family as a whole was marked by turmoil and uncertainty.

Jung looked for a way out of his loneliness and instability by carving, at 10 years old, a 6-centimetre male with a 'frock coat, with unusually tall hat and shiny black boots' (Jung, 1989, p. 9) in a ruler, colouring it with black ink and putting it in a spring box with a crib, along with a smooth, oblong blackish stone from the Rhine, which he painted colourfully so that an upper and a lower half emerged. He hid this male in the screed of the house, where he was forbidden to go. After that he felt safe. No one could discover or destroy his secret. He felt safe, and the tormenting sense of disunion with himself was gone.

Already in this symbolic act one might suspect the influence of the archetypal image of the grandfather, especially when you know that frock and cylinder were garments from the nineteenth century. This symbol of the male had probably archetypal force for Jung and awakened expectation and hope. As he grew older, he carved an enlarged male in stone – as

'Atmavictus' (Breath of Life') – and put the stone in his garden in Küsnacht. It symbolized, as the ruler, male vitality.

When he was 11 years old, the family moved to Basel and Jung attended the local high school. He felt that his parents, compared with his schoolmates, were not powerful, rich or distinguished, but poor and the importance of his pastor father was low. He described in his memoirs that he thought when he went to Basel as a poor high school student, a part of him was important, of great authority, powerful and influential:

> a high authority, a man not to be trifled with, as powerful and influ-
> ential as this manufacturer. This 'other' was an old man who lived in
> the eighteenth century, wore buckled shoes and a white wig and went
> driving in a fly with high, concave rear wheels between which the
> box was suspended on springs and leather straps.
>
> (Jung, 1989, p. 29)

In addition, in high school he was looked upon as the 'grandson of Dr. Jung' and not as the pastor's son Carl (Bair, 2003, p. 58).

Jung mentioned other stories that showed him in puberty that he actually belonged to the eighteenth century. The many stories he had heard from his parents and relatives on his paternal grandfather were connected with this feeling, he suggested. He expressed this to Aniela Jaffé in the memories (only published in German), saying he was a strong and striking personality. A great organizer, tremendously active, brilliant, witty and eloquent. He himself was still swimming in his wake. 'Professor Jung was something!' it was said in Basel. His children were very impressed by him. They not only worshipped him, but were afraid of him, for he was a somewhat tyrannical father (Jaffé, 1990, p. 404). During the afternoon nap of a quarter of an hour, his family had always to sit quiet as a mouse at the table. He had authority, which his father lacked.

It is therefore conceivable that Jung, compensating for the insignificance of his parents in those years of puberty, in which self-discovery and the search for a role model are central, found an ideal one in his famous grandfather. Perhaps this grandfather gave him the required vitality, the 'Atmavictus' and the creativity that he missed in his father's abstract words; the grandfather complex gave him an internal working model, an orientation, expectation patterns and emotions such as hope and strengths, and since he had not himself known the grandfather, this image could develop an archetypal image, not tested against the reality.

It may also be that his father, who was weak in face of his own father, delegated the creative power to his son. C.G. Jung would therefore live the thwarted impulses of his father. Children identify with such unconscious impulses. They receive 'orders'; roles are delegated to them (Stierlin, 1975). The creative power and vitality of the grandfather was certainly impressive for the grandson.

As it was rumoured, this grandfather was a son of Goethe, so the identification with the grandfather was 'easier'. Jung told Jaffé that assumedly Sophie Ziegler gave birth to an illegitimate son of Goethe, and this was his grandfather, Carl Gustav Jung (Jaffé, 1990, p. 399). Jaffé wrote that Jung mentioned this reported legend with a certain complacency (Jaffé, 1990, p. 400). Jung had been fascinated by Goethe's *Faust*, and this could now be understood: Faust held, as Jung, two souls in his chest. On the other hand, Jung described the rumour as 'annoying' and 'bad taste' (Jaffé, 1990, p. 400). Jung told this story to Jaffé in old age, from an objective distance. What role did the legend have for the young Jung?

It can be assumed that this 'secret' of its origin exerted a strong attraction on the imaginative young Jung and supported the archetypal effect of a grandfather image. Deidre Bair mentions in a comprehensive biography of Jung that he boasted as a youth of his relationship with Goethe as an ancestor. She describes an incident in which his cousins from the maternal line of the Preiswerks stressed their nobility and celebrity (his maternal grandfather was Samuel Preiswerk, Antistes of Basel). C.G. Jung seemed annoyed about that. Anyway, he led in 1894, as a 19-year-old, his cousins to a statue of his grandfather, which had been set up in Basel, and asked them to watch exactly the revered grandfather in order to recognize the similarity between him and Goethe. The Preiswerks were impressed, as Jung had intended. He told them that the man with the buckled shoes, who often drove from the Black Forest with him to Kleinhüningen with his old-fashioned carriage, was none other than Goethe (Letter of Zumstein-Preiswerk to Ellenberger, 28 January 1975, cited in Bair, 2003, p. 667).

That he thought a part of him was alive in the eighteenth century, powerful and important, and was of great authority, wore buckled shoes and moved a carriage, suggests that Jung identified with his grandfather/Goethe and thus on the paternal line much more than on the maternal line. This process was supported by the family myth of a relationship with Goethe. Fears, uncertainty and loneliness, anger and shame about his weak father could be moved and managed by referring back to the ancestral lineage.

When it came to choosing a career, Jung initially could not decide. He was interested in both the natural sciences and the humanities, such as history and philosophy. It felt like a dead end, as he had two dreams that pointed him towards medicine. This came, strangely enough, not to his mind previously, he said to Jaffé, although his paternal grandfather was a doctor of whom he had heard so much. However, that was also the reason why he had some resistance to this occupation. He didn't want to imitate – this was his motto (Jung, 1989, p. 81). He consciously wanted to search for his own way, but his unconscious advised him to follow the footsteps of his grandfather. He finally opted for medical studies.

His grandson, the historian and architect Andreas Jung, supported the view of the strong connection of Jung with his paternal grandfather, and that he was a role model (A. Jung, 2011, p. 659). Andreas Jung, who manages the family archive and lives in the home of C.G. Jung in Küsnacht, found striking parallels in the lives of both men. He compared quotes from C.G. Jung's memoirs with quotes from the diary of his grandfather, C.G. Jung. In Andreas Jung's eyes the parallels are not only amazing, but almost mystical:

> Both their fathers were born into big families with about a dozen brothers and sisters from different mothers, and both were the second to last born. In contrast the two of them grew up in small families and had only one younger sister, who never married. The marriages of both their parents were unfortunate; their fathers were stuck in their profession and had a meagre income, their mothers were depressed. Both were close to their mothers, but the relationship with their fathers was difficult. They both studied medicine at the local university. After their diplomas they moved away to the capital town, where they were to start a brilliant university career. But after severe difficulties they left everything behind and started a new life in another environment in their scientific work. In addition, they had a private medical practice, gave lecturers and wrote several books. Both married young ladies belonging to the upper class. They had many children: each had a son who became a talented architect, and a daughter, who was a gifted semi-professional singer.
>
> (A. Jung, 2011, p. 663)

If one agrees with Andreas Jung, the effect of the archetypal image of the grandfather on the individuation of the grandson is impressive. However, it must be said, the impact of the maternal line of spiritualistic interest cannot be underestimated, but shall not be pursued further, since the image of his paternal grandfather helped Jung much more to build a persona, a professional role and a male identity than did the maternal line.

Jung chiselled, towards the end of his life in 1955/6, his paternal ancestors on three stone tablets, and painted the ceiling of the Loggia, among others, with motifs from his coat of arms. Originally, the paternal line had a phoenix as its heraldic animal, which symbolized 'young', 'youth' and 'rejuvenation'. C.G. Jung said in his memoirs that his grandfather had changed the coat of arms, probably in opposition to his father, and because he had been a Freemason and Grand Master of the Swiss Lodge. Carl Gustav Jung, the grandfather, had removed the phoenix as an emblem.

> Instead there is now a cross azure in chief dexter and in base sinister a blue bunch of grapes in a field d'or; separating these is an estoile d'or in a fess azure. The symbolism of these arms is Masonic, or Rosicrucian.
>
> (Jung, 1989, p. 232)

The cross and grape were the symbols of the heavenly and the chthonic spirit. The Golden Star was the symbol of the gold of the philosophers (Jung, 1989, p. 232). The Rosicrucian was the successor of alchemical philosophy. Jung assumed his grandfather had known alchemists, as at that time pharmacology was still strongly under the influence of Paracelsus and thus under alchemical influence. Jung once more grouped together with his grandfather; he himself devoted much to alchemical studies.

This delegation he mentioned in old age. When chiselling of pedigrees he thought:

> I became aware of the fateful links between me and my ancestors. I feel very strongly that I am under the influence of things or questions which were left incomplete and unanswered by my parents and grandparents and more distant ancestors. It often seems as if there were an impersonal karma within a family, which is passed on from parents to children. It has always seemed to me that I had to answer questions which fate had posed to my forefathers, and which had not yet been answered, or as if I had to complete or perhaps continue, things which previous ages had left unfinished.
>
> (Jung, 1989, p. 233)

C.G. Jung mentioned the fact that his own individuation process was influenced by the ancestors and their delegations. The archetypal effect of the positive spirit of his grandfather was underpinned by family myths, his celebrity and the shared name; he represented a better role model than the father.

References

Adjaye, J.A., & Aborampah, O.M. (2004). Intergenerational cultural transmission among the Akan of Ghana. In E. Larkin, D. Friedlander, S. Newman & R. Goff (Eds), *Intergenerational relationships: Conversations on practice and research across cultures* (pp. 23–39). New York: Haworth Press.

Afanasyev, A. (2013). *Russian fairy tales*. Ebook. Planet.

Ainsworth, M., Blehar, M., Waters, E., & Wall, S. (1978). *Patterns of attachment: Assessed in the strange situation and at home.* Hillsdale, NJ: Erlbaum.

Attar-Schwartz, S., Tan, J.-P., Buchanan, A., & Flouri, E. (2009). Grandparenting and adolescent adjustment. *Journal of Family Psychology, 23*(1), 67–75.

Bair, D. (2003). *C.G. Jung: A biography.* Boston, MA: Little, Brown & Company.

Barrows, A. (2004). Athers and families: Locating the ghost in the nursery. *Infant Mental Health Journal, 25*(5), 408–423.

Barthes, R. (2010). *Camera Lucida. Reflections on Photography*, Reprint edition. Transl. by R. Howard. New York: Hill and Wang.

Bédier, J. (1945). *The romance of Tristan and Iseult.* Unknown author. Transl. by H. Belloc. New York: Pantheon Books.

Beebe, B., & Lachmann, F.M. (2002). *Infant research and adult treatment: Co-constructing interactions.* Hillsdale, NJ: Analytic Press.

Beland, R., & Mills, T. (2001). Positive portrayal of grandparents in current children's literature. *Journal of Family Issues, 22*, 639–651.

Bengtson, V.L. (1985). Diversity and symbolism in grandparental roles. In V.L. Bengtson & J.F. Robertson, *Grandparenthood* (pp. 11–25). Beverly Hills, CA: Sage Publications.

Benjamin, J. (2004). Beyond doer and done to: An intersubjective view of thirdness. *Psychoanalytic Quarterly, 73*, 5–46.

Benjamin, W. (1940 [2003]). *Selected Writings: 1938–1940.* Vol. 4, ed. H. Eiland, M.W. Jennings. Cambridge, MA: Harvard University Press.

Bergmann, S., Jucovy, M.E., & Kestenberg, J.S. (1995). *Kinder der Opfer: Kinder der Täter. Psychoanalyse und Holocaust.* Fischer: Frankfurt/Main.

Betz, O. (2000). Der Einsiedler als Ratgeber. In U. Heindrichs & H.A. Heindrichs (Eds), *Alter und Weisheit im Märchen: Forschungsberichte aus der Welt der Märchen* (pp. 267–281). Kreuzlingen: Diederichs.

Birkhäuser-Oeri, S. (1977). *Die Mutter im Märchen. Deutung der Problematik des Mütterlichen und des Mutterkomplexes am Beispiel bekannter Märchen.* Stuttgart: Adolf Bonz.

Bisagni, F. (2009). Transference and the non-total situation. In F. Bisagni, N. Fina, & C. Vezzoli (Eds), *Jung today: Childhood and adolescence.* Vol. 2 (pp. 5–22). Hauppauge: Nova Science Publisher.

Bovensiepen, G. (2006). Attachment-dissociation network: Some thoughts about a modern complex theory. *Journal of Analytical Psychology, 51,* 451–466.

Bovensiepen, G. (2009). Depressive Komplexorganisation und narzisstische Störung. *Analytische Psychologie, 156*(1), 37–56.

Bovensiepen, G. (2011). C.G. Jung heute: Der analytische Prozess. *Analytische Psychologie, 165*(3), 288–312.

Bowlby, J. (1969). *Attachment and loss.* Vol. 1: *Attachment.* London: Hogarth Press.

Bowlby, J. (1973). *Attachment and loss.* Vol. 2: *Separation: Anxiety and anger.* London: Hogarth Press and the Institute of Psychoanalysis.

Brecht, B. (1939/2013). Die unwürdige Greisin. In *Kalendergeschichten* (pp. 114–120). Berlin: Suhrkamp.

Bruschweiler-Stern, N., Lyons-Ruth, K., Morgan, A.C., Nahum, J.P., & Sander, L.W. (2007). The foundational level of psychodynamic meaning: Implicit process in relation to conflict, defense and the dynamic unconscious. *International Journal of Psychoanalysis, 88,* 1–16.

Cambray, J. (2010). Emergence and the self. In M. Stein (Ed.), *Jungian psychoanalysis: Working in the spirit of C.G. Jung* (pp. 53–66). Chicago, IL: La Salle, Open Court.

Cambray, J., & Carter, L. (2004). Analytic methods revisited. In J. Cambray & L. Carter (Eds), *Analytical psychology: Contemporary perspectives in Jungian analysis* (pp. 116–148). Hove: Brunner-Routledge.

Caputo, R.K. (2001). Grandparents and coresident grandchildren in a youth cohort. *Journal of Family Issues, 22*(5), 541–556.

Cavalli, A. (2012). Transgenerational transmission of indigestible facts: From trauma, deadly ghosts and mental voids to meaning-making interpretations. *Journal of Analytical Psychology, 57*(5), 597–614.

Chase Goodman, C., & Silverstein, M. (2001). Grandmothers who parent their grandchildren. *Journal of Family Issues, 22*(5), 557–578.

Colman, W. (2013). Reflections on knowledge and experience. *Journal of Analytical Psychology, 58*(2), 200–218.

Connolly, A.M. (2011). Healing the wounds of our fathers: Intergenerational trauma, memory, symbolization and narrative. *Journal of Analytical Psychology, 56*(5), 607–626.

Creuzer, F. (1819–23). *Symbolik und Mythologie der alten Völker, besonders der Griechen: (6–6)*, 2nd revised edition. Leipzig und Darmstadt: Heyer + Leska.

de Beauvoir, S. (1997). *Die Alten*. Hamburg: Reinbeck.

Deacon, T.W. (2003). Multilevel selection in a complex adaptive system: The problem of language origin. In R.H. Weber & D.J. Depew (Eds), *Evolution and learning: The Baldwin effect reconsidered* (pp. 81–106). Cambridge, MA: MIT Press.

Dieckmann, H. (1991). *Komplexe. Diagnostik und Therapie in der analytischen Psychologie*. Berlin: Springer Verlag.

Diederichs, U. (1955) (Ed.). *Russische Volksmärchen*. Düsseldorf-Köln: Diederichs.

Dieterich, M. (2001). *Einführung in die Allgemeine Psychotherapie und Seelsorge*. Wuppertal: Brockhaus.

Donde, A. (1989) (Ed.) *Little Red Riding Hood: A casebook*. Madison, WI: University of Wisconsin Press.

Drell, M.J. (2005). A matter of context: Who says there can't be friendly ghosts? *Infant Mental Health Journal, 26*(6), 521–524.

Drew, L.M., & Silverstein, M. (2007). Grandparents' psychological well-being after loss of contact with their grandchildren. *Journal of Family Psychology, 21*(3), 372–379.

Duggin, R. (2008). Ghosts in the nursery and wolves at the door. *Infant Observation, 11*(1), 5–15.

Ellenberger, H.F. (2011). *Die Entdeckung des Unbewussten: Geschichte und Entwicklung der dynamischen Psychiatrie von den Anfängen bis zu Janet, Freud, Adler und Jung*, transl. G. Theusner-Stampa, new edition. Zürich: Diogenes.

Ennulat, G. (2000). Die Großmutter im Märchen. In U. Heindrichs & H.A. Heindrichs (Eds), *Alter und Weisheit im Märchen: Forschungsergebnisse aus der Welt der Märchen* (pp. 76–88). Kreuzlingen: Diederichs.

Faimberg, H. (2005). *The telescoping of generations: Listening to the narcissistic links between generations*. London: Routledge.

Fordham, M. (1985). *Explorations into the self*, Vol. 7. London: Karnac.

Fraiberg, S. (1980). Ghosts in the nursery: A psychoanalytic approach to the problem of impaired infant–mother relationships. *Clinical Studies in Infant Mental Health: The First Year of Life* (pp. 164–196). London: Tavistock Publications.

Fraiberg, S., Adelson, E., & Shapiro, V. (1975). Ghosts in the nursery: A psychoanalytic approach to the problem of impaired infant–mother relationships. *Journal of American Academy of Child Psychiatry, 14*, 387–422.

Georgaca, E. (2001). Voices of the self in psychotherapy: A qualitative analysis. *British Journal of Medical Psychology, 74*, 223–236.

Gotthold, J.J., & Sorter, D. (2006). Moments of meeting: An exploration of the implicit dimensions of empathic immersion in adult and child treatment. *International Journal of Psychoanalytic Self Psychology, 1*(1), 103–119.

Graf, P., & Schacter, D.L. (1985). Implicit and explicit memory for new associations in normal and amnesic subjects. *Journal of Experimental Psychology, Learning, Memory and Cognition, 11*(3), 501–518.

Green, A. (2011). *Die tote Mutter: Psychoanalytische Studien zu Lebensnarzissmus und Todesnarzissmus*, 2nd edition. Giessen: Psychosozial Verlag.

Grimm, J., & Grimm, W. (2014). *The original folk and fairy tales of Grimm Brothers.* The complete first edition. Shine Classics, CreateSpace Independent Publishing Platform.

Gross, P. (2013). *Wir werden älter. Vielen Dank. Aber wozu? Vier Annäherungen*, 4th edition. Freiburg: Herder.

Hank, K., & Buber, I. (2007). *Grandparents caring for their grandchildren: Findings from the 2004 Survey on Health, Ageing and Retirement in Europe.* Mannheim: Mannheim Research Institute for the Economics of Ageing.

Haule, J.R. (2011). *Jung in the 21st century.* Vol. 1: *Evolution and archetype.* London: Routledge.

Hendriks-Jansen, H. (1996). *Catching ourselves in the act: Situated activity, interactive emergence, evolution and human thought.* Cambridge, MA: MIT Press.

Hillmann, H. (1983). *Archetypal psychology. A brief account.* Woodstock, CT: Spring Publications.

Hogenson, G.B. (2004a) Archetypes: Emergence and the psyche's deep structure. In J. Cambray & L. Carter (Eds), *Analytical psychology: Contemporary perspectives in Jungian analysis* (pp. 32–56). Hove: Brunner-Routledge.

Hogenson, G.B. (2004b). What are symbols symbols of? Situated action, mythological bootstrapping and the emergence of the Self. *Journal of Analytical Psychology, 49*(1), 67–81.

Hogenson, G.B. (2005). The Self, the symbolic and synchronicity: Virtual realities and the emergence of the psyche. *Journal of Analytical Psychology, 50*(3), 271–284.

Hogenson, G.B. (2009). Archetypes as action patterns. *Journal of Analytical Psychology, 54*(3), 325–337.

Holzberg, N. (2007). *Ovids Metamorphosen.* München: C.H. Beck.

Hooyman, N., & Kiyak, H.A. (1988). *Social gerontology: A multidisciplinary perspective.* Boston, MA: Allyn & Bacon.

Höpflinger, F., Hummel, C., & Hugentobler, V. (2006). *Enkelkinder und ihre Großeltern: Intergenerationale Beziehungen im Wandel.* Zürich: Seismo.

Hüsken, K., Seiz, K., Tautorat, P., Walter, M., & Wolf, K. (2008). *Kinderbetreuung in Familien. Abschlussbericht*, ed. by Deutsches Jugendinstitut. Dortmund: Technische Universität.

Jacobi, J. (1959). *Complex. Archetype. Symbol in the psychology of C.G. Jung.* Transl. Ralph Manheim. New York: Bollingen Foundation.

Jacobi, J. (1973). *The psychology of C.G. Jung: an introduction with illustrations*. Transl. Ralph Manheim. New Haven, CT: Yale University Press.

Jaenicke, C. (2006). *Das Risiko der Verbundenheit: Intersubjektivitätstheorie in der Praxis*. Stuttgart: Klett-Cotta.

Jaffé, A. (1990). Einiges über C.G. Jungs Familie. In Jung, C.G., *C.G. Jung, Erinnerungen, Träume, Gedanken von C.G. Jung*, ed. by Aniela Jaffé, 7th edition (pp. 399–407). Olten: Walter-Verlag.

Jung, A. (2011). The grandfather. *Journal of Psychology, 56*(2), 653–673.

Jung, C.G. (1911). On the doctrine of complexes. In *Experimental researches*. Appendix, *Collected works 2* (pp. 598–604). Transl. by R.F.C. Hull. 2nd edition. Princeton, NJ: Princeton University Press. (All further references to Jung's *Collected works*, abbreviated *CW* will be with the chapter, book title, volume of *CW*, and page numbers.)

Jung, C.G. (1912). *Symbols of transformation, CW 5*.

Jung, C.G. (1916). The transcendent function. In *The Structure and dynamics of the psyche, CW 8* (pp. 67–92).

Jung, C.G. (1919). The psychological foundations of belief in spirits. In *The structure and dynamics of the psyche, CW 8* (pp. 301–318).

Jung, C.G. (1925). *Introduction to Jungian psychology: Notes of the seminar on analytical psychology given in 1925*. Transl. by W. McGuire & R.F.C. Hull. Princeton, NJ: Princeton University Press.

Jung, C.G. (1928). On psychic energy: General remarks on the energic point of view in psychology. In *The structure and dynamics of the psyche, CW 8* (pp. 3–66).

Jung, C.G. (1929). Problems of modern psychotherapy. In *The practice of psychotherapy, CW 16* (pp. 53–76).

Jung, C.G. (1934a). A review of the complex theory. In *The structure and dynamics of the psyche, CW 8* (pp. 92–106).

Jung, C.G. (1934b). The relations between the ego and the unconscious. In *Two essays on analytical psychology, CW 7* (pp. 123–243).

Jung, C.G. (1935). Principles of practical psychotherapy. In *The practice of psychotherapy, CW 16* (pp. 3–20).

Jung, C.G. (1942). On the psychology of the unconscious. In *Two essays on analytical psychology, CW 7* (pp. 3–122).

Jung, C.G. (1945) The phenomenology of the spirit in fairytales. In *The archetypes and the collective unconscious, CW 9/1* (pp. 207–254).

Jung, C.G. (1946). The psychology of transference. In *The practice of psychotherapy, CW 16* (pp. 163–326).

Jung, C.G. (1947). On the Nature of the Psyche. In *The structure and dynamics of the psyche, CW 8* (pp. 159–234).

Jung, C.G. (1950). *Aion: Researches into the phenomenology of the self. CW 9/2*.

Jung, C.G. (1952). Synchronicity: An acausal connecting principle. In *The structure and dynamics of the psyche, CW 8* (pp. 417–532).

Jung, C.G. (1989). *Memories, dreams, reflections*, ed. by A. Jaffé. Transl. R. Winston & C. Winston. 4th edition. Vintage Books: New York.

Jung, C.G. (2009). *The red book: Liber novus*, ed. by S. Shamdasani. W.W. Norton: New York.

Kahana, B., & Kahana, E. (1970). Grandparenthood from the perspective of the developing grandchild. *Developmental Psychology, 3*(1), 98–105.

Kalsched, D. (1996). *The inner world of trauma: Archetypal defenses of the personal spirit*. London: Routledge.

Karmiloff-Smith, A. (1992). *Beyond modularity: A developmental on cognitive science*. Cambridge, MA: MIT Press.

Kast, V. (1985). *Der Teufel mit den drei goldenen Haaren. Vom Vertrauen in das eigene Schicksal*. Freiburg: Kreuz.

Kast, V. (1992). *The dynamics of symbols: Fundamentals of Jungian psychotherapy*. Transl. Susan A. Schwarz. New York: Fromm Intl.

Kast, V. (1994). *Väter-Töchter, Mutter-Söhne, Wege zur eigenen Identität aus Vater- und Mutterkomplexen*. Stuttgart: Kreuz.

Keller, L., & Bechstein, L. (1954). *Der alte Zauberer und die Kinder*. Wien: Waldheim-Eberle.

Knox, J. (2003). *Archetype, attachment, analysis: Jungian psychology and the emergent mind*. Hove: Brunner-Routledge.

Knox, J. (2012). Selbstwirksamkeit in Beziehungen: das Selbst aus interpersoneller Sicht. *Analytische Psychologie, 170*(43), 450–471.

Kohut, H. (1966 [1978]). Forms and transformations of narcissism. In P. Ornstein (Ed.), *The search for the self*, Vol. 1 (pp. 427–460). Madison, CT: International Universities Press.

Krieger, N.M. (2014). *Bridges to consciousness: Complexes and complexity*. Hove: Routledge.

Lachmann, F. (2008). The process of transforming. *International Journal of Psychoanalytic Self Psychology, 3*(1), 1–15.

Laub, D. (1998). The empty circle: Children of survivors and the limits of reconstruction. *Journal of the American Psychological Association, 46*, 507–529.

Lieberman, A. (1999). Negative maternal attributions: Effects of toddlers' sense of self. *Psychoanalytic Inquiry, 19*(5), 737–754.

Lieberman, A.F., Padro'n, E., Van Horn, P., & Harris, W.W. (2005). Angels in the nursery: The intergenerational transmission of benevolent parental influences. *Infant Mental Health Journal, 26*(6), 504–520.

Lussier, G., Deater-Deckard, K., Dunn, J., & Davies, L. (2002). Support across two generations: Children's closeness to grandparents following parental divorce and remarriage. *Journal of Family Psychology, 16*(3), 363–376.

Lyons-Ruth, K. (1998). Implicit relational knowing: Its role in development and psychoanalytic treatment. *Infant Mental Health Journal, 19*, 282–289.

Maennersdoerfer, M.C. (2000). Von Elementargeistern, Dämonen und anderen alten Gelichter. In U. Heindrichs & H.A. Heindrichs (Eds), *Alter und Weisheit im Märchen. Forschungsberichte aus der Welt der Märchen* (pp. 141–155). Kreuzlingen: Diedrichs.

Mallet, C.-H. (1987). Kennen Sie Kinder? *Wie Kinder denken, handeln und fühlen. Aufgezeigt an vier Grimmschen Märchen*. München: dtv.

Marcel, A.J. (1988). Phenomenal experience and functionalism. In A.J. Marcel & E. Bisiach (Eds) *Consciousness in contemporary science*. Oxford: Clarendon Press.

Martin-Vallas, F. (2006). The transferential chimera: A clinical approach. *Journal of Analytical Psychology, 51*(5), 627–642.

Martin-Vallas, F. (2008). The transferential chimera: Some theoretical considerations. *Journal of Analytical Psychology, 53*(1), 37–59.

Martin-Vallas, F. (2013). Are archetypes transmitted or emergent? A response to Christian Roesler. *Journal of Analytical Psychology, 58*(2), 278–285.

Massing, A., Reich, G., & Sperling, E. (2006). *Die Mehrgenerationen-Familientherapie*. Göttingen: Vandenhoeck & Ruprecht.

Mbele, J. (2004). The elder in African society: The view from folklore and literature, intergenerational cultural transmission among the akan of ghana. In E. Larkin, D. Friedlander, S. Newman, & R. Goff (Eds), *Intergenerational relationships: Conversations on practice and research across cultures* (pp. 53–61). New York: Haworth Press.

Meier, I. (2013). Complexes and schemas: A comparison of the concepts of analytical psychology based on work of C.G. Jung and the schema therapy of Jeffery Young. *International Journal of Psychotherapy, 17*(3), 71–79.

Meltzer, D., & Harris Williams, M. (1988). *The apprehension of beauty*. Perthshire: Clunie Press.

Meredith-Owen, W. (2013). Are waves of relational assumptions eroding traditional analysis? *Journal of Analytical Psychology, 58*(5), 593–614.

Moore, R., & Gillette, D. (1991). King, warrior, magician, lover: Rediscovering the archetypes of the mature masculine. New York: HarperOne.

Neppl, K.J., Ontai, L.L., & Conger R.D. (2010). Grandmother involvement as a protective factor for early childhood social adjustment. *Journal of Family Psychology, 24*(5), 635–645.

Orange, D.M. (2004). *Emotionales Verständnis und Intersubjektivität*. Frankfurt/Main: Brandes & Apsel.

Orange, D.M., Atwood, G.E., & Stolorow, R.D. (2001). *Intersubjektivität in der Psychoanalyse: Kontextualismus in der psychoanalytischen Praxis*. Frankfurt/Main: Brandes & Apsel.

Otscheret, L. (2005). Dialektik ohne Dialog. Intersubjektivität bei C.G. Jung. In L. Otscheret & C. Braun (Eds) *Im Dialog mit dem Andern: Intersubjektivität in Psychoanalyse und Psychotherapie* (pp. 57–83). Frankfurt/Main: Brandes & Apsel.

Otscheret, L., & Braun, C. (Eds) (2005). *Im Dialog mit dem Anderen. Intersubjektivität in Psychoanalyse und Psychotherapie*. Frankfurt/Main: Brandes & Apsel.

Perelberg, R.J. (1997). Introduction to Part I. In J. Raphael-Leff & R.J. Perelberg (Eds) *Female experience*. London: Routledge.

Perrault, C. (1697). *Contes de Perrault*. Genf: Slatkine Reprints.

Pickering, J. (2012). Bearing the unbearable: Ancestral transmission through dreams and moving metaphors in the analytic field. *Journal of Analytical Psychology, 57*(5), 576–596.

Rauwald, M. (Ed.) (2013). *Vererbte Wunden. Transgenerationelle Weitergabe traumatischer Erfahrungen*. Weinheim: Beltz.

Reich, G., Massing, A., & Cierpka, M. (2007). *Praxis der psychoanalytischen Familien- und Paartherapie*. Stuttgart: Kohlhammer.

Riedel, I. (1995). *Die weise Frau in uralt-neuen Erfahrungen*. München: dtv.

Riedel. I. (2006). Frau Holle. *Wie aus einer ungeliebten Tochter eine starke Frau wird*. Freiburg: Kreuz.

Roesler, C. (2012a). Archetypen: Ein zentrales Konzept der Analytischen Psychologie. *Analytische Psychologie, 43*(4), 487–510.

Roesler, C. (2012b). Are archetypes transmitted more by culture than biology? Questions arising from conceptualizations of the archetype. *Journal of Analytical Psychology, 57*(2), 224–247.

Roesler, C. (2013). Das gemeinsame Unbewusste: Unbewusste Austausch- und Synchronisierungsprozesse in der Psychotherapie und in nahen Beziehungen. *Analytische Psychologie, 44*(4), 464–487.

Ruiz, S.A., & Silverstein, M. (2007). Relationships with grandparents and the emotional well-being of late adolescence and young adult grandchildren. *Journal of Social Issues, 63*, 793–808.

Saunders, P., & Skar, P. (2001). Archetypes, complexes and self-organization. *Journal of Analytical Psychology, 46*(2), 305–323.

Schlegel, D., & Schlegel, F. (1804). *Geschichte des Zauberers Merlin*, 2nd edition. München: Eugen Diederichs Verlag.

Schwob, P. (1988). *Großeltern und Enkelkinder: Zur Familiendynamik der Generationsbeziehung*. Heidelberg: Asanger.

Schwob, P. (1990). Großeltern, Eltern, Kinder: Liebe – und was noch? In P. Buchheim, M Cierpka, & Th. Seifert (Eds), *Lindauer-Texte: Texte zur psychotherapeutischen Fort- und Weiterbildung* (pp. 62–76). Berlin: Springer.

Shalit, E. (2002). *The complex: Path of transformation from archetype to ego*. Toronto: Inner City Books.

Siegel, D.J. (2012). *The developing mind. How relationships and the brain interact to shape who we are*, 2nd edition. New York: Guilford Press.

Silverstein, M. (1866). *The story of Aladdin or the wonder-lamp*. Quedlinburg: G. Basse.

Spyri, J. (2007, 1899). *Heidi: Her years of wandering and learning*. Transl. by H. James Dole. Raleigh, NC: Hayes Barton Press.

Stern, D. (2000). *The interpersonal world of the infant: A view from psychoanalysis and developmental psychology*. New York: Basic Books.

Stern, D. (2004). *The present moment in psychotherapy and everyday life*. New York: W.W. Norton.

Stevens, A. (1982). *Archetypes: A natural history of the self.* New York: William Morrow & Co.

Stevens, A. (2003). *Archetype revisited: An updated natural history of the self.* Toronto: Inner City Books.

Stevens, A., & Price, J. (1996). *Evolutionary psychiatry: A new beginning*. London: Routledge.

Stierlin, H. (Ed.) (1975) *Von der Psychoanalyse zur Familientherapie*. Stuttgart: Klett-Cotta.

Thelen, E., & Smith, L. (1998). *A dynamic systems approach to the development of cognition and action*. Cambridge, MA: MIT Press.

Timberlake, E.M. (1980). The value of grandchildren to grandmothers. *Journal of Gerontological Social Work, 3*(1), 63–76.

Tolkien, J.R.R. (1991). *Lord of the Rings*. London: Harper Collins.

Tresan, D.I. (1996). Jungian metapsychology and neurobiological theory. *Journal of Analytical Psychology, 41*(3), 399–436.

Trevarthen, C. (1999/2000). Musicality and the intrinsic motive pulse: Evidence from human psychobiology and infant communication. *Musicae Scientiae, 3*, 155–215.

Uhlendorff, H. (2003). Großeltern und Enkelkinder: Sozialwissenschaftliche Perspektiven und Forschungsergebnisse hinsichtlich einer selten untersuchten Beziehung. *Psychologie in Erziehung und Unterricht, 50*, 111–128.

Volkmann, H. (2000). Die Alten in '1001 Nacht'. In U. Heindrichs & H.-A. Heindrichs (Eds), *Diederichs Alter und Weisheit im Märchen. Forschungsberichte aus der Welt der Märchen* (pp. 109–123). Kreuzlingen: München.

von Eschenbach, W. (2003). *Parzival*. Transl. by P. Knecht, 2nd edition. Berlin: Walter de Gruyter.

von Franz, M.-L. (1977). *Das Weibliche im Märchen*, 12th revised edition. Leinfelden-Echterdingen: Bonz.

von Franz, M.-L. (1991). *Der Schatten und das Böse im Märchen*. München: Knaur.

Weber, B.H. (2003). Emergence of mind and the Baldwin effect. In B.H. Weber & D.J. Depew (Eds), *Evolution and learning: The Baldwin effect reconsidered* (pp. 309–326). Cambridge, MA: MIT Press.

Weber, B. (2013). Sterbebegleitung für ein Kind. *Tages-Anzeiger*, 25 November 2013.

Wieland-Burston, W. (2010). 'Bubbe Mayseh' (the archetype of grandparents), or me and my grandparents: Stories and history. In M. Stein & Raya A. Jones (Eds), *Cultures and identities in transition, Jungian perspectives* (pp. 41–53). New York: Routledge.

Zuckerman, B., & Zuckerman, P. (2005). The pediatrician as ghostbuster: Angels voices and kisses. *Infant Mental Health Journal, 26*(6), 529–532.

Index